W9-DIE-641

I AM THE HOLY LAND

... and so are you

I AM THE HOLY LAND

… and so are you

Fr. Leo P. Maxfield, M.S.

AVALINI

I AM THE HOLY LAND ... *and so are you*
Copyright © 2007 by La Salette of Enfield, Inc., P.O. Box 420,
Enfield, NH 03748

All rights reserved. Printed in the United States of America.
No part of this book may be used or reproduced, stored or
transmitted in any manner whatsoever without written
permission from the Publisher, except in the case of brief
quotations embodied in critical articles and reviews.

Recorded and transcribed by Doreen Couture. Edited by Fr.
Stephen L. White and Clare Karis.

Cover Photo: The La Salette cross on the steeple of the retreat
house at the La Salette shrine, Attleboro, MA.

All biblical quotations are from The New American Bible
(Copyright © 1991, 1986, 1970 Confraternity of Christian
Doctrine, Inc., Washington, DC) unless otherwise noted.

ISBN-13: 978-0-9715270-4-1
ISBN-10: 0-9715270-4-0

First Edition
ABCDEFGHIJK

Published by
AVALINI
1343 Main Street
Fitchburg, MA 01420

For more information about us, please contact
AVALINI, 1343 Main Street, Fitchburg, MA 01420
or visit us at www.avalini.com.

CONTENTS

EDITOR'S NOTE

The Feast of the Epiphany, 2007
Princeton, New Jersey

Anyone who knows Fr. Leo Maxfield knows what a wonderfully gifted storyteller he is. As a young boy I can remember him visiting our home and telling stories in French, which I did not understand, to the assembled adults. But from his facial expressions and the movement of his hands I was as entertained as the adults were who understood French. His style of speaking is equally distinctive and captivating and I have tried to preserve as much of this as possible as I edited the stories he told to Dori Couture which she recorded and transcribed in 2004 and 2005. Of course there is no way to preserve his unique facial expressions and hand gestures in the written word, but those who know him will easily be able to imagine them as they read.

Fr. Leo calls what follows his memoirs and most of these stories do indeed construct a picture of his life and priestly ministry. But, as he insists throughout, these stories are not really so much about him as they are about how God works in the world and how powerful prayer can be. Mixed in here and there are homilies, Bible meditations, and mini sermons, and even a review of a book that further illustrate Fr. Leo's lifelong wonder and amazement at God's love for each one of us.

Most of the stories are what we might call "feel good" stories that give us a warm, intimate glimpse of how a person's deep and abiding faith changed him or someone else, often through healing of a spiritual or physical malady. Some of the stories show another side of reality that is often hidden from our eyes, namely the way the forces of evil attempt to divert us from our relationship with God. Indeed, those who strive most vigorously for union with God in this life are often the most vulnerable to those evil forces, as these stories will show.

Many people have heard nearly all of these stories in one setting or another and those who know Fr. Leo will have no trouble believing them. But those who have not had the blessing of knowing him and of sitting with him as he relates his personal experiences that show the power of prayer may be challenged by some of the stories here. Some of them are, in the truest sense of the words, incredible and unbelievable. Some are so incredible and unbelievable that a few people who have never met Fr. Leo or who do not know him well may be tempted to think that these stories are made up in order to make a larger point. I myself am usually highly critical and skeptical of seemingly far-fetched stories and, while I believe in the *possibility* of miracles and manifestations of evil powers that are at war with God's people, I also believe they are exceedingly rare.

As understandable as such a reaction might be, I want to attest that Fr. Leo is as credible a person as one could ever hope to meet. He is not a fanatical person given to flights of fancy fueled by religious fervor. He is, instead, a man with both feet planted firmly on the ground and a man of faithful prayer who has had the courage to allow his heart and mind to be open to the mysterious ways God can relate to those who have "eyes to see and ears to hear." It should be noted that Fr. Leo himself found many of the things he learned incredible when he first encountered them and it is only his openness to how God can surprise and startle us that allowed him to go deeper into a profound ministry of healing through prayer and utter trust in God's love and mercy.

And so I invite each one of you to do what Fr. Leo did when he was offered the opportunity—the grace—to be touched by the Holy Spirit. Open your hearts and minds to God and don't be afraid. For it was not only in biblical times, but in our own time as well, that we can see God's "signs and wonders" all around us.

These stories would never have been assembled but for the insistence of Dori Couture that Fr. Leo allow her to record them. For many years his friends and family have urged him to get these stories down on paper, but finally it was Dori's persistence and hard work that have made them a reality. Our debt to her is immense.

Fr. Stephen L. White

I AM THE HOLY LAND ... *and so are you*

To my parents, Arthur and Antoinette, who first gave me my faith and then showed me how to live it.

My parents and me at St. Cecilia's Church, Leominster, Massachusetts, May 29, 1955, the day after my ordination to the priesthood, just after my first Mass.

La Salette Shrine
Enfield, New Hampshire
On the 50th Anniversary of my
Ordination to the Priesthood

✠

✠

"...you will receive power when the Holy Spirit comes upon you, and you will be my witnesses in Jerusalem, throughout Judea and Samaria, and to the ends of the Earth."

~ Acts of the Apostles 1:8

"A king's secret it is prudent to keep, but the works of God are to be declared and made known. Praise them with due honor."

~ Tobit 12:7

"Write down all these things that have happened to you."

~ Tobit 12:20

"We are talking about God; so why are you surprised if you cannot grasp it? I mean, if you can grasp it, it isn't God!"

~ St. Augustine of Hippo

✠

ON GOD'S MOUNTAIN

Five minutes can make such a difference in a person's life. Five minutes on the top of Mount Horeb in the Sinai Desert (also known as Mount Sinai where Moses encountered God in the burning bush) on March 22, 1978 changed mine forever—or at least consolidated some changes in me that had been shaping and forming me all my life until then.

While I was in Rome on a sabbatical leave in 1977-78 a good friend gave me money to do something I might like. There was a trip to the Holy Land that was being organized specifically for priests and seminarians. I spoke to my Superior in Rome and asked permission to go, which he readily granted. We left the week before Palm Sunday for Tel Aviv.

I was so happy to go where all the great stories in the Bible take place—the Holy Land. I was going to be where Jesus and Mary had been. I just *knew* it was going to be a wonderful, beautiful experience and I was very excited.

When we got to Tel Aviv and got off the plane I thought, "I'm finally in the Holy Land!" I looked around and I was in an airport and there were taxis and buses and people running with suitcases and I said, "Well, I've seen all this before. I've got to get out of this airport and find out what this Holy Land looks like." We got on a bus and drove all the way to Bethlehem the first day. Our guide, who was Fr. Robert North from the Biblical Institute, knew the Holy Land like the palm of his hand and he would point things out to us: "Over here is where Rachel is buried," he would say, "And over there is where Samson slew the Philistines." I'd look out the window and all I would see were fields with rocks and some bushes and I'd think, "It doesn't look like anything special to me."

We got to Bethlehem and we got off the bus and went to the church built over the place where they say Jesus was born. It was down some stairs into something like a cave. I was moved to think that Jesus was born there but it really didn't mean all that much to me since it looked so ordinary. We came out of the church and right away these young men came running up to us trying to sell us all kinds of souvenirs made there in the Holy Land. It was all so commercial and I didn't expect it to be like this. I was disappointed.

We got back on the bus and drove to the outskirts of Jerusalem. It was getting dark and our guide pointed out Jerusalem and the walls surrounding the city. As I was looking at the walls around Jerusalem on our way to Bethany where we were to spend the night, it didn't mean very much to me. The next day, we saw where they think Martha, Mary and Lazarus lived and the tomb where Lazarus had been buried when called out by Jesus. Again, it didn't move me at all, at least not in the way that I expected. That same day we went to the place where Jesus was supposed to have started his walk into Jerusalem on Palm Sunday when they threw the palms in front of him and cried, "Hosanna." There were a lot of people there—Palm Sunday—and we started the procession from there into Jerusalem. I noticed in the crowd there were some young men trying to pick pockets and I warned everybody in my group to be careful. I thought, "And here in the Holy Land guys are picking pockets!" That was a disappointment too.

We saw many other places mentioned in the Bible. But everything I saw seemed ordinary and some of it was even ugly, like picking pockets and selling souvenirs. Nothing about the Holy Land looked at all beautiful.

The next day we boarded the bus for the two-day trip to the Sinai Desert. It was an old bus and we had to cover our mouths and noses because of the dust in the desert. I don't know what I expected, but it wasn't this. In movies I had seen deserts with nice white sand and dunes but this was just a lot of dust and rock and little, dry bushes, and little hills that were all dried up. I wasn't surprised that the people of Israel thought about looking for another God after wandering around here for 40 years.

Finally we reached Mount Sinai—also called Mount Horeb—where God gave Moses the Ten Commandments. As we climbed we saw the cave where Elijah was when God passed by—just a hole in the hill. From time to time I would look back down at the desert that was all kind of gray and ugly. I was feeling so disappointed with my whole experience so far. We finally got to the top of the mountain. As some of the others were getting everything ready to celebrate Mass on the summit, I left the group and went off by myself behind some rocks where I could be alone and nobody could see me. As I sat there I said, "Lord, is this really the Holy Land? Lord, I'm sorry. I'm having trouble believing this is the Holy Land. Lord, I could think of so many other places better than this for a Holy Land. Everything I've seen since I got here is either very ordinary or even ugly, and, I'm sorry, Lord, but I'm having trouble."

Mt. Sinai—a forbidding place.

Then all of a sudden I heard a voice somewhere inside me, I guess. It said, "Leo, look at yourself." And I stopped and I looked at myself, deep within myself. I saw the same thing. I saw an ugly desert, a dry desert. I saw a life, which wasn't anything very spectacular, just kind of ordinary. In many ways ordinary and in other ways pretty ugly. And then the voice continued, "But you know that *you* are the Holy Land, because the only thing that makes this land holy is that I came. And you're looking for everything but me. And I came to you too, so *you're* the Holy Land."

Wow! I sat there for a moment thinking about this. "*I'm* the Holy Land! *I'm* the Holy Land!" It doesn't make any difference if everything in my life is ordinary and ugly. He came and he's with me. He came to me and he came to make *me* holy. I'm the Holy Land because he came and that's all that matters.

I jumped up and I ran back to the group getting ready for Mass and I wanted to scream to everybody, "Hey, guess what? *I'm* the Holy Land! *You're* the Holy Land. *We're* the Holy Land." Oh, that Mass was so beautiful.

Later I practically flew down that mountain, running and jumping all the way down. I was the Holy Land and God is so good. When we got back to the bus I opened my Bible and I came upon Chapter 35 of Isaiah, where it says "Let the wilderness and the dry lands exult..." As you go on reading it says, "God is coming...the eyes of the blind shall see." It continues "...for water gushes in the desert, streams in the wasteland..."[1] That was just such a great experience for me that I have to keep thinking about it every now and again. So, anytime I feel a little bit down, I think, "Hey wait a minute now! I'm the Holy Land."

In a way this story sets the stage for a telling of everything that has happened in my ministry, before and after that wonderful day on Mount Horeb. It's a story about how we *all* are the Holy Land.

BEGINNINGS

"You are my God, I thank you." Many times have I prayed these words from Psalm 118 while saying the daily office. Sometimes after praying familiar words over and over, they take on a new meaning or a special significance. And so it

---

[1] Isaiah 35:1, 4-6 in the *Jerusalem Bible* translation.

was that one day I realized this was the only prayer I really needed. No more needs to be added; anything else would be beside the point. He is *my* God and so I am his. What else to do except give him thanks?

I remember how Jesus said in the book *He and I*, the famous account of Gabrielle Bossis' dialogues with Jesus:[2] "Time is not enough for me; I need eternity with which to love you." And *we* will need eternity with which to thank him.

My family in the summer of 1946. I'm the second from the right, second row.

As my health declines and I face the possibility of meeting and thanking God face to face, I now think so often of the wonderful things he has done in my life, of the good people I have met and the powerful experiences I have had. As I review my life I am amazed that God has chosen to use me in

---

[2] Gabrielle Bossis, *He and I*. Sherbrooke, Québec: Editions Paulines, 1969.

some extraordinary ways to heal bodies and souls. The thing is, it's not me or anything about me, but God working in me that causes me so much wonder. This is very important to remember as you read these stories: this is not about me, but

about God working in me. And here is something else to keep in mind: God wishes to work through each one of us in amazing ways if only we let him. In order that I might say as the Virgin Mary said: "For the Mighty One has done great things for me; And holy is his name."[3] I have tried to set down some of the experiences of my life and ministry that others may rejoice with me and say "He is my God, I thank him."

I am the seventh of fifteen children of devout French-Canadian Catholic parents from Leominster, Massachusetts. The neighborhood where we lived was called "French Hill" and the wonderfully peculiar French-Canadian Catholic culture permeated every aspect of our lives. Services in Saint Cecilia's Church were all in French and the nuns in the parish school, several of them from France, taught us classes in both French and English. Everything was centered around family and the church and my parents taught us our prayers and helped us grow in the faith from as early as any of us can remember.

---

[3] Luke 1:49. This is, of course, from the song of Mary that we call the *Magnificat*. It is always said as part of Vespers, the daily evening prayers of the Church.

As a boy I enjoyed sports and also scouting with all of the outdoor activities. As I remember, I had earned 19 merit badges before I left for the seminary at fifteen years of age. That was in 1944.

More about that later. But I do need to skip ahead for a story. While driving back to Leominster from Fall River,  Massachusetts with my parents after my ordination my mother said: "I want to tell you something. When I was pregnant with you 25 years ago, I went to church; and before the statue of the Virgin Mary, I said: 'Mary, if this is a boy I am carrying, I would like him to be a priest, and to be yours.' And today you became a priest and a missionary of Our Lady of La Salette, and so my prayer was answered." And so I learned that God listens to mothers' prayers for their children.

As the years have gone by, I have often remembered those words of my mother and wondered why she would have prayed that way when expecting me, the seventh of her fifteen children. Then one day, it dawned on me that a year and two months before I was born, my mother's father died in a very tragic way.

He was a barber and had his shop directly across the street from the present parish church. It seems that the owner of the building wanted to raise the rent on his shop. My grandfather didn't know how he could pay that amount and still support his wife and children and he went into a deep depression. On March 24, 1928, he was seen on a bridge over the Nashua River on Mechanic Street looking down into the river and a moment later, he was seen falling. No one knows for sure if he fell or jumped but it was judged to be a suicide. I know what a shock it must have been to my mother.

I was her next pregnancy. I was born on May 31, 1929. As a priest, thinking back, I could very well imagine that she would pray that if she were carrying a boy, he would be a priest. In the Old Testament, Nazarites were sons consecrated to God by their parents and set apart from others for some special purpose. Samson was a Nazarite.[4] I guess I was too, although I doubt my mother would have known that word or what it meant. And if she did, I don't think she would have applied it to any of her children!

But that never occurred to me as I was growing up. What I do remember is that occasionally my mother would say, "I hope at least one of my boys will be a priest." I must have wondered if it might be me. I don't believe I was more pious or devout than any of my siblings, or any of my friends. I do remember the nuns at school sometimes asking if I ever thought of being a priest. But then again, they probably asked many of the boys the same question. If the priesthood is a certain kind of vocation—a calling—then God must use other people to utter his words, like my mother and the nuns. I wonder if we have lost this precious way of participating in God's calling the young to his work in the church.

In any case, there certainly were events in my life that made me think more seriously about God and religion. One of these was what happened to my godfather, my uncle Leo Maxfield, after whom I was named.

To understand why the following was memorable and significant, you must remember that I was one of many brothers and sisters. We all had the same parents but we each had our own godparents. That alone made them special, not only the fact that they paid special attention to us and gave us an occasional coin. One fact, unknown to my family at the time, is that my godfather once took me aside and made me promise I would never smoke. That may seem trivial, but to me, it was important. I knew from this how much he cared about me.

On August 5, 1940, he committed suicide. I was eleven years old and at the time I was spending two weeks at

---

[4] See the Book of Numbers, chapter 6, Judges 13:5,7;16:17

Boy Scout Camp in Jaffrey, NH, as a cub scout. I was not told about his death.

One day after I had returned home, I was on our front porch with some of my siblings and a cousin. The conversation turned to godparents and what they did for us. I bragged about what my godfather would do for me. The cousin retorted, "No he won't. He's dead. He shot himself." The usual "give and take" of young children ensued: "He did not," "He did too," "He did not," "Oh yeah, well ask your mother." I ran into the house and said: "Mom, Doris said that Uncle Leo shot himself. It isn't true, is it?" She didn't answer. She only looked at me and I knew it was true.

I ran out of the house and all the way to the cemetery to the Maxfield family plot where I fell on the ground and wept bitterly, crying out: "Why? Why did you do this?"

It affected me deeply but I don't remember it making me think of being a priest. However, it did make me think of life and death and must have led me more deeply into prayer.

Life continued despite this emptiness. I did well in school and became more involved in scouting and in sports, especially baseball, which I loved. Being a young boy, I dreamed of someday being a great baseball player.

In the eighth and final year of grammar school, I began to think of high school. I was told I would have a choice of courses depending on what I might want to choose as a career. That same year, a few representatives of religious communities came to speak to us eighth graders about their schools or seminaries. That, and some occasional literature about the priesthood and religious life, got me thinking more seriously about my vocation. But not enough to keep me from deciding to enter the only Catholic high school in the area, St. Bernard's in Fitchburg, Massachusetts.

I didn't think my parents could ever afford to send me to college, so rather than take a classical course, I decided on a commercial course. That year in high school, the war year 1943-1944, was mostly uneventful. I enjoyed it, and besides the studies, I began to play basketball. There were several of us from my parish in Leominster who attended St. Bernard's and, though we ranged from freshmen to seniors, we got along well together and went to sporting events and dances together. I can truly say it was an enjoyable year.

But we were growing up and not in as protective an environment as we had known in grammar school. I began to hear stories and jokes that didn't seem appropriate for Christian young people. It surprised me and got me to thinking about what I might do about it. Suddenly, I found myself surmising that if I were a priest, I *could* probably do something to help remedy the situation. Now, what had only been an occasional thought of mine, or suggestion of someone else, became stronger and stronger. Still, life in high school was a happy time and I couldn't imagine exchanging it for seminary life. It took a rather dramatic event to bring about that decision.

Perhaps my best friend at the time was a boy a year older than I named Paul Paquet. We were completely into scouting and sporting events together. I hope he enjoyed my company as much as I enjoyed his. Paul had some serious health problems. The most serious, as I remember, was an asthmatic condition. In any case, at one point he was hospitalized and I was told there was fear for his life. One night I went to Leominster Hospital to see him. I was told that since I was not family, I could not see him. I would not be deterred. I went around to the back door and found my way to his room. When I entered, only his parents were there. Paul was propped up in bed and breathing with much difficulty. He didn't know me. My best friend seemed to be dying and he didn't know me. I ran out of the hospital, fell on the lawn away from everyone and everything and there in the dark, I sobbed and sobbed and I said, "Lord, if you let him live, I will really think seriously about becoming a priest." Well, he got better, and so I did what I had promised.

CALLING

Not long after Paul recovered it came to me clearly that I was being called by God to be a priest. I'm not sure I can remember exactly how I knew this or if I could explain it even if I could remember. But after a while I was pretty certain this is not only what God wanted me to do, it was also what I wanted to do. So my next step was deciding what seminary I would enter. Having studied in Catholic schools, I had been told about different religious orders of priests and brothers and I had been given literature about a few of them. I also had a friend and former neighbor, Charles Dube, who had moved into St. Joseph's parish in nearby Fitchburg. The parish was staffed by the La Salette Missionaries and so after he finished the eighth grade in their grammar school, he went off to their seminary in Hartford, Connecticut. He kept in touch with me and joining him seemed an obvious choice. He sent me their recruiter, Fr. Joseph Higgins.

Fr. Higgins visited me and gave me the necessary papers to fill out. I needed a letter from the pastor of my parish, Fr. Joseph Chicoine (pictured here). Conversations with him were always in French. My father came along with me when I approached him about a letter.

Fr. Chicoine explained to us that the La Salette Missionaries had another seminary in Enfield, New Hampshire, this one for boys who spoke French. Why not conserve my French language and go there?" he asked. I hesitated, thinking of my friend at the seminary in Hartford. "Wait a few days," Fr. Chicoine said, "Fr. Eugene Mills from the Enfield, NH seminary will be here visiting his family in the parish."

Within a few days, Fr. Mills showed up at my home. He didn't try to change my mind about Hartford, he only told me about the La Salette Seminary in Enfield. It was on a lake, surrounded by hills, had ball fields, a gymnasium and a huge farm. It sounded appealing. I decided to go there and soon received the necessary papers. The La Salette Seminary in Enfield turned out to be a dream place and made the strict discipline and hard studies easier to take. Enfield has been my home ever since.

The La Salette Shrine at Enfield, NH where I entered the order and where I live now.

After five years in Enfield, I went to the Novitiate in East Brewster, Massachusetts to prepare for vows which I took in July 1950. Then on to La Salette Seminary in Attleboro, Massachusetts to study philosophy and theology. On May 28, 1955 I was ordained a priest in St. Mary's Cathedral, Fall River, Massachusetts.

Celebrating my first Mass at St. Cecilia's in Leominster, Massachusetts.

It was after that ceremony, as we drove home, that my mother told me what I related earlier, that when I was in her womb, she had said a prayer that I might become a priest and belong to Mary. I felt very much in God's hands; and in the heart of the Virgin Mary to whom the cathedral church where I had just been ordained was dedicated.

A YOUNG PRIEST

After ordination I still had to finish a year of theology in Attleboro. Then, in 1956, I was assigned to help with the business matters of our French language publication *Celle Qui Pleure*.[5] My job was to go to the French-speaking communities around New England to speak in parish churches on Sundays and try to get people to subscribe to our publication.

Frankly, I did not enjoy that work, but fortunately it did not last long. After a year working with *Celle Qui Pleure*, I was assigned as Vocational Director. I would visit schools in French-speaking parishes to try and recruit candidates for our La Salette Seminary in Enfield. Because of that work, I was often invited to give talks and even retreats in many schools, both grammar and high. I enjoyed this work very much.

But there was one drawback. All the work I had been given to do since my ordination had required a lot of traveling and I began to feel a need to settle down. In the Fall of 1963 I was given the opportunity to go to Rome for three months for what was called a semester, a sort of "Sabbath time" for priests of my religious congregation. I jumped at the chance.

On my way to Rome with three other La Salette priests, we were able to visit a good part of Europe. Then we settled down at our General House in Rome for prayer and study. One day, feeling very zealous, I went to our Superior

---

[5] "She Who Weeps." In her apparition at La Salette in France in 1846, the Virgin Mary had appeared weeping.

General and offered my services for any of our foreign missions. I was sure I would be sent to Madagascar or Argentina or the Philippine Islands. Instead he said he needed another priest at the new La Salette Seminary in Spain. It had been opened a few years earlier to recruit vocations for possible work in South America. Since I had offered my services for wherever I was needed, I accepted. And so from 1964 to 1983 I lived and worked in Spain.

SPAIN

Our school in Spain was in the little village of Santa Maria de Nieva, about twenty miles from the provincial capital of Segovia. There I taught boys aged 12 to 18 to prepare them for further studies that would lead to their ordination. In 1969 I was sent to the city of Valladolid where there were several seminaries run by various religious orders and the local diocese. I set up a house for our boys to live in while they attended classes in the various seminaries. They initially took basic college courses before specializing in philosophy, and then went on to study theology.

My life in Spain was very different from my life in America, but it was uneventful, especially after I got to Valladolid. A La Salette brother and I lived with the boys, but the boys went off every day after Mass for classes, not returning until dinner time. So there wasn't much for me to do during the day. At first I spent a lot of time alone and eventually got involved teaching English at a nearby girls school. But life was pretty uneventful and, to tell the truth, maybe even a little boring. Then in 1974 I returned to the States for a vacation and from that summer on my life would never be the same.

What happened? When my niece was confirmed in Denver the Bishop told all the confirmands "How I wish I could make you understand that after tonight everything is possible." I had been confirmed many years earlier, and ordained a priest in 1955, but it took an experience on July 16, 1974 to make me understand that which I should have known, that in the Name of Jesus Christ and through the power of the Spirit all things are possible. This is why I want to tell the story of my ministry—so that all Christians and, especially priests, will come to understand that better; knowing as I do, that many of them have much to teach me as well.

While I was in Spain I began to hear about something called the Charismatic Renewal movement and I was curious to learn more. I finally found a Jesuit priest in the city where I was who was interested in Charismatic Renewal and wanted to know more about it. I went to see him and he said, "Yes, I've heard about it. I met a couple from Madrid who started a group down there. I thought it might be interesting to start a group here." So I suggested that we start right there at the Jesuit house.

This priest had called me in the spring before I went home on vacation saying he had a priest visiting from Australia who spoke Spanish too. The Australian priest wanted to talk with my Jesuit acquaintance about Charismatic Renewal and he thought I would like to meet him. I was eager to meet someone with whom I could speak English for a change!

So I went over and I waited until he was finished speaking with the Jesuit priest. Then he came out and we were introduced. He said, "I'm very sorry that I don't have time to really talk with you. I've got to catch a train back to Madrid." So I offered to drive him to the station. On the way to the train station I asked him why he had come. He said he wanted to learn about Charismatic Renewal. I told him I'd heard about it and that I'd read somewhere about these groups in the states and some of the colleges and universities getting into prayer groups where they claim to sing in tongues. And he said, "Yeah, that's right. That's what we're talking about." My reaction was that I didn't want to hear any more about such things because they seemed crazy to me. Just before I left him at the train he said "Listen, get a book by Father O'Connor on Charismatic Renewal. It's very good."

Not long after that I took a group of young people, along with some of my seminarians and some of the people in the parish where I was helping, on a trip to Toledo on the bus. We wanted to leave early but it was Sunday and we needed to have Mass. I wondered aloud what to do, and one of the boys who was from a village about a quarter of the way to Toledo said, "I'm sure the pastor in my hometown will let us use the church." He called ahead to make arrangements for us.

We stopped and I said the Mass in the church for the people. I thought there was something special about that Mass, but I wasn't sure what it was. I just felt very fervent. Then we got back on the bus and went to Toledo. When we got into Toledo and parked, everybody was eager to see the sights of this beautiful city. But I had been there before and had seen all those things. So I told them when and where to meet up later in the afternoon for the return trip home and then went off by myself.

As I walked up a narrow cobblestone side street all of a sudden I saw a doorway that looked like a doorway to a church or monastery right in the middle of all these buildings. I was curious so I went down a couple of steps and then through a big wooden door and entered a beautiful chapel. There was no one there, but in the back there were some bars and, I noticed, some cloistered nuns. They had a convent in the back and they could come out on the other side of the bars and one would come out and pray for a while. I walked into that chapel and got in one of the pews. I was all by myself and I started praying. I still didn't know how to pray; it was before I learned much about Charismatic Renewal or had any experiences of my own. But for some reason, I just felt very comfortable being there, talking to God about all kinds of things. A couple of hours went by. Suddenly people started to come in and they pretty much filled the church. Then Mass started.

After Mass was over everybody left, but I stayed there. In all, I was there at least four hours, and I was not a bit tired. I thought, "This was the first time in my life that I had ever prayed straight for four hours and not been tired. What in the world is happening to me? I came out of the church and went back to the bus just as the kids were arriving. As we drove back I felt as though something happened or something was happening, but I couldn't tell what—it was very confusing. This was just before I returned to the States and went up to Burlington. I think that church experience was a kind of preparation but I didn't realize it at the time except for that Australian priest telling me that I should read more about Charismatic Renewal.

RENEWAL

Before I came home from Spain in the summer of 1974, a nun I knew, who was working in Vermont, wrote to me to tell me about a house of prayer they called "Hope" (an acronym for House of Prayer Experience) in Burlington. She invited me to come to spend a few days and since as a religious I was required to make a retreat every year anyway, I gladly accepted.

When I arrived I found that my friend was giving a Bible study that afternoon. This surprised me because I knew her when she was just in high school and now here she was teaching the Bible and doing a very good job. After the Bible study and supper, maybe about 7:00 o'clock or so, I was invited to evening prayer with everybody who was there. I remember there was a room with chairs in a circle and they gave me a book with some Psalms. They began to sing. I noticed that several of them had their hands up—arms raised up as they were singing and this struck me as rather unusual. I wasn't used to seeing people praying and singing with upraised arms. And I must say it made me very uncomfortable.

After we sang, we sat down. A Psalm book was passed around and we each took turns reading verses. After each person read we would stop and someone would say aloud something like this, "Lord, I want to thank you for this day and we praise you with this Psalm, and praise you with all the saints and angels." Whatever they would think of they would say. Then somebody else would say, "I too want to thank you" for this and that. At one point someone said, "Thank you, Lord, for sending Fr. Leo today." This made me feel very uncomfortable. I had never prayed like this in public, expressing inner thoughts and feelings so openly. I felt embarrassed and uncomfortable with this whole experience, with its moments of silence, and moments of singing and moments of reading Psalms or other prayers. My discomfort only increased as the hour wore on.

The next morning there was morning prayer that was quite similar to the previous evening's format. Later in the morning there was a Mass. Again, I felt that everyone was quite demonstrative at Mass with their arms up and singing and so forth. Nonetheless, it struck me that the Mass was particularly beautiful. The priest who was saying the Mass was Fr. Gerry Ragis and the words he had to say were very meaningful. Later that afternoon I had one of my really bad headaches which I had from time to time. I mentioned this to my friend and she said, "Oh, well, if you want to go lie down, go right ahead. You don't need to come to any of the exercises we are having." I was so relieved, in spite of my awful headache. What a relief it was not to feel I had to go to another one of those awkward prayer meetings! I was glad to get out of being with them and seeing them raise their hands and all the rest of the "antics" they were doing when we were praying. I didn't realize at the time that this was what they called Charismatic Prayer.

I skipped supper that night and the next morning one of the nuns who was a friend of my friend, came over and said, "How are you feeling this morning?" I said, "Oh, I'm okay now." Then she said she had left a magazine on my desk— each guest had a desk. She also said she had left a book for me and then said, "If you'd like, before you leave, we could pray with you about your headaches." That made me feel very uncomfortable because it sounded as though she were saying, "We're going to pray with you and you won't have any more headaches." or "We're going to do a little miracle here." I didn't understand this at all. I quickly went to my desk and saw there the magazine, *New Covenant*, put out by the Charismatic Renewal. That particular issue was all about healing so I began to read the articles. I read about how people were getting into charismatic prayer, praying for healings and actually seeing all kinds of healings.

I found this fascinating. Then I looked at the book that was also on my desk. It was called *The Lord is my Shepherd*. Each chapter was by a different priest who was saying how charismatic prayer changed his whole life. They found so much more joy in life and a deeper love for prayer. Even their faith grew and they felt full of hope. Of course, this appealed to me, but I was still skeptical. One of the priests who had written a chapter in *The Lord is my Shepherd* was the same Gerry Ragis who was right there at the House with me. He certainly seemed like a normal enough person. So I began to wonder what this Charismatic Renewal was all about.

I began to read whatever I could find concerning Charismatic Renewal. One was a book called, *The Cross and the Switchblade,* the true story of the start of David Wilkerson's ministry to gang members in New York City and the conversion of Nicky Cruz, a notorious gang leader.[6] I read this book very quickly. It was later made into a movie starring Pat Boone.

A day or so later the nuns told me there was going to be a Charismatic prayer group meeting at Rice High School in Burlington and asked if I would like to go. Feeling a bit wary I asked, "Will this be one of these groups where they speak in tongues and give prophesies and that kind of thing I've been reading about?" They said, "Well, that does happen!" I then thought, "Well I'd like to see this; see what this is all about." I was surprised that I was really pretty eager to go and to see what would happen. So the nuns drove me over to Rice High School. When we walked into the gym there was somebody

---

[6] Grand Rapids, Michigan: Chosen Books, 2000.

sitting at a desk and they brought me over and had me put on a name tag. Many people came over and greeted me, all so happy they were hugging me. At that time in my life I couldn't believe that people could be so happy about coming to pray.

We went into the gym and sat down in a circle. There must have been 200 people there sitting in different rows in circles waiting for the prayers to begin. It began when everybody stood up to sing a song. Everybody in the gym raised their arms up high. Everybody, that is, except me, of course, because I still felt so uncomfortable with such a demonstration.

After a while, however, I thought, "I'd better try to imitate them." So, I cautiously put my hands up and opened my hands a little bit. But, I couldn't get them very much higher than my sides. After a couple of songs, we sat down and somebody got up and welcomed everyone and then looked over my way and said, "We have some new people here tonight. Nice to see you." And then he said, "You know why we're here. Let's not waste time. We're here just to praise God. So let's do that. Let's praise God." He sat down and all of a sudden everybody but me began to pray spontaneously out loud saying things like, "I praise you, Lord," "I thank you, Lord," and "I love you and adore you and thank you for this day" and thank you for this and thank you for that and praise you for this and praise you for that. I was becoming extremely uncomfortable. So I just sat there and listened to it all. Then they stopped and there was silence.

Then out of the silence I heard a voice and the voice said something like, "My people. I thank you for coming here tonight to praise me. Continue to praise me and I will bless you." I looked over and saw a woman who was saying that. I thought, "Well who does she think she is, God?" This happened four or five times during the two hours that we were there, where somebody would suddenly speak out loud, as if God were speaking. This made me even more uncomfortable and even somewhat troubled.   And then there was more silence. After a while, out of the silence, I began to hear what sounded like a murmuring. From the murmuring came what sounded like singing, yet I couldn't understand anything. I couldn't make out any words because it seemed to be a combination of a lot of languages. Instead of making me uncomfortable as the prayers and other utterances had made me, this struck me as really rather beautiful. It sounded like harmonized singing. In any case, I found it a little spooky but also nice. I honestly didn't know what to think.

All of this went on for two hours and nobody had left, which I thought was rather amazing—that people would pray for two hours and nobody would walk out. I had been to many Masses at which people left right after receiving communion and nobody stayed after the Mass was finished. But here, everyone seemed to want this to just keep going on and on.

On the way back to Hope after the prayer group ended, my friend's friend, Sister Mary, said: "Well, what did you think of the prayer meeting?" I said, "Well, Sister, everybody was there praying and I guess I can't knock that, but I don't think this is for me." She said, "What did you think of the prophecies?" And I said, "What prophecies?" Then she said, "Well, don't you remember when somebody would speak out loud in God's name?" And I said, "Oh you call that prophecy?" She said, "Well, yes, what's a prophet in the Bible, but someone who speaks in God's name? Not necessarily someone who tells you the future, but someone who speaks in God's name." So I said, "Well, yes, I guess you're right." She said, "Well, that's all. That's all they were doing." I said, "I know, but I could start saying something like that too. How would you know it was prophecy?" She said, "Well, you don't understand. They don't say it because they want to; they say it because they have to." She said, "It happened to me once. I had to open my mouth. I had these words in my mouth and I had to open it and let it all come out."

I was having a hard time believing all this. It seemed so strange and alien to me, and it was deeply unsettling. Then Sister Mary said, "What did you think of the tongues?" And I said, "Is that what you call singing in tongues when I couldn't understand anything and everybody was apparently humming or singing in different languages." She said, "Yes." And I said, "I have to admit it really sounded beautiful, but I found it a little spooky, I guess." So then I said, "Anyway, let's go home."

When we got back to the House it was getting late so I went to bed. I don't know what time it was, but in the middle of the night I suddenly sat up, wide awake. I sat straight up in bed as though I knew something was going to happen. Then I heard a voice so clear, and the voice said, "This *is* my prayer." And I thought, "Where did that voice come from?" Even to this day, I really can't say if the voice came from outside of me or inside of me. All I know is that it was so clear, and it said, "This *is* my prayer."

Ordinarily, if I heard something like that in the middle of the night I would be rather frightened and nervous and have trouble going back to sleep; but this time I lay back in bed, pulled the sheets up and the next thing I knew, it was morning. My first thought was of hearing the voice in the middle of the night saying, "This is my prayer." Well, I thought to myself, "I'm not going to tell anybody about that. I don't know if I'm dreaming or what's going on here. I do know I heard a voice, but I'd better keep quiet about it."

So I didn't say anything about this for a long time. I called home and told my mother that I was going to stay at this Prayer House for several more days because I had to look into something. I was supposed to go home on Friday, but I stayed over until the following Thursday because I wanted to go back to the prayer group on Wednesday at Rice High School. In the meantime, I kept reading books and asking questions. The idea behind tongues, as it was explained to me, is that, "Doesn't it ever happen to you that you want to say something but you can't find the words? Even if you wanted to tell someone you loved them. You could say, 'I love you. I adore you.' What else? Maybe you'd like to say more than that but you don't have the words to say anything more. Tongues is really the Holy Spirit helping you say what you can't say because you can't find the words. But God knows what you're trying to say, what you're trying to express. The Holy Spirit knows and wants you to express what you can't find words to express." That sort of made sense to me.

I tried to keep an open mind about everything that was happening to me even though a lot of it didn't make any sense. I was still very skeptical. On Monday after the first Wednesday at Rice High School, I was rather convinced that there was something to this Charismatic Prayer. I yearned for what all these other priests said they found; a life of deeper prayer, more joy in my vocation, more faith, and a love for the word of God. I thought these are all wonderful things and I wanted all of it.

On Tuesday morning I went to see Fr. Gerry Ragis and I said, "You know I've been reading about this Charismatic thing and I think I would like to be prayed over, or what I think you call, Baptism in the Spirit. I think I'd like that." And he said, "I heard that you were asking a lot of questions and doing a lot of reading so I guess you know pretty much what it's all about." And he said, "Let me just ask you, do you want to receive the gifts of the Holy Spirit?" And I said, "No, no, I don't want that." I said, "I don't want to talk in tongues or prophecy and all that. I just want to have more joy in my vocation, more faith, and more prayer—that kind of thing. I can skip the gifts." And he said, "Well, wait a minute now." And he opened the Bible to St. Paul's first letter to the Corinthians, Chapter 14 verse 1. Paul says, "Pursue love, but strive eagerly for the spiritual gifts, above all that you may prophesy." "See?" said Fr. Ragis, "Paul is saying right here, ask for the gifts. Do you believe this is the word of God?" And I said, "Yes." And then he said, "Well, how can you say you don't want them when Paul is saying to ask for them?" Well, I didn't know how to answer that so I shrugged and said, "Well, all right, okay, I suppose."

He invited me to come that very evening before the prayer group, and said they would pray with me then. I was hoping he would say tomorrow or the day after; I didn't know it was going to be so soon! But I couldn't back out now.

I spent a miserable day thinking, "I can't do this." I kept thinking what my family would say when I got home and told them I was prayed over to be touched by the Holy Spirit. I figured they would say, "I thought you already had the Holy Spirit at Baptism and Confirmation and Ordination." Which is true and it's what I would have said before all this happened to me. What would they say when I told them I'm into this movement where they pray in tongues? They'll think I'm crazy. I think I'm not going to go. I think I'll tell him I've changed my mind. But whenever I felt that way I would go to the Chapel and pray, especially to Mary, and I'd feel better and I'd renew my determination to go through with it. I didn't realize at the time but I really think now that the devil was trying to get me to change my mind. I really believe that.

GIFTS

After a day of agonizing, I went to the prayer group after supper. I was the first one there. Fr. Ragis came in and he had called a few other people and they came in and he said, "We're here because Fr. Leo would like us to pray for him for Baptism of the Spirit." And they all smiled and said, "Oh, that's wonderful." I wasn't too sure it was wonderful, but they sure thought it was. He put a chair in the middle of the room and asked me to sit down but I told him I wanted to kneel instead. So I knelt down and everyone gathered around me. There must have been seven or eight people and they all laid their hands on me. I didn't expect that and it made me want to jump up and run out and say, "Take your hands off of me. The Bishop laid his hands on me and ordained me a priest. What are you going to do? What do you want to give me that I haven't already got?" But instead I felt I should be humble because I don't have all the answers.

They began to pray for me and I closed my eyes and I began to pray saying silently, "You know, Mary, I think you're the one who got me to come in here, so please help me now."

And all of sudden, with my eyes closed, I saw her. I know it was like a dream, but it was more than a dream. I saw a beautiful woman and I knew for certain—dream or no dream—that it was Mary. I couldn't make out her face very well because she was bathed in light. But she reached over and took me by the hand and in that moment it seemed as though we were running along a mountainside with green grass and wildflowers everywhere. Both of us were running faster and faster, and the wind was blowing and blowing, and I thought, "I can't run this fast, I'm going to fall." But she had me by the hand and I kept going. Then, all of a sudden she was gone and I was back and I knew where I was. But I also knew that Jesus was right there by my side. I never saw anything of him but I felt his presence right there by my side as real as anything I've ever experienced. I have never felt the presence of Jesus Christ as I did at that moment and it was as if Mary had brought me to him and said, "Okay, here he is." Again, it was about a year before I told anybody this because I thought, "They're going to think I'm crazy, or it's all my imagination and how do I know it's not? Maybe I was dreaming." Yet, I knew it was more than a dream, much more than a dream.

Was this a dream, or was it something else? More importantly, was it real? I wondered about this for a long while. Back in Spain I met a very holy nun who was the Superior in a cloistered convent. After I got to know her I told her of my experience running with Mary as I was prayed over. She told me that St. Theresa of Avila—and St. Thomas Aquinas before her—called such an experience "a vision of the imagination," a real vision, but where God speaks to you through your own imagination. It is real but it is not an apparition, or a sensing of something physically present. She told me that St. Theresa says that God can speak to us that way. She continued, "Well, that was all that it was—no big thing." Aquinas says "The essence of God is not seen in a vision of the imagination; but the imagination receives some form representing God according to some mode of similitude; as in the divine Scripture divine things are metaphorically described by means of sensible things."[7]

What I thought was such a big thing and wasn't ready to tell anybody, she thought was fairly run of the mill. And she was in good company! St. Theresa of Avila and St. Thomas Aquinas, and who knows who else among the saints have written about such things. In any case, I'm sure Jesus was there. I knew that and I just started to speak to him in silence and I began to say, "Oh Lord, I'm sorry that I hesitated so much. I'm sorry. And now here I am. Fill me with your Spirit. Give me anything you want. I'll take anything you want now. If you want to give me those gifts I didn't want—tongues, and prophecy and healing and all the others…" I began to name all these gifts.[8] "…Discernment, and wisdom and knowledge. If you want to give me those, I'll take them." I knelt there saying this in silence. Suddenly, my friend, the nun, who had her hands on my head or shoulder, began speaking: "I will give you everything you ask for and more than you ask for." She was saying aloud the exact words I was uttering to God in silence! I was amazed.

A couple of days later I asked her what made her say the words she spoke. She said, "I don't know. It was just that all of a sudden I had it in my mouth, and when I opened my mouth that sentence came out, 'I will give you everything you ask for and more than you ask for.'" So, I said, "You know what? At that very same time I was asking the Lord to give me all kinds of things. Then you said what you said. So, I want to thank you, saying the words that I was saying silently."

When the prayers over me ended I got up off my knees and hugged everybody. Suddenly I was really full of joy and enthusiasm. It was time for evening prayer with the rest of the people so we went back to that room where we had been before in the circle. This time, much to my own surprise, *I* was the first one to raise his arms in praise and song. I wanted to

---

[7] *Summa Theologica*, I, xii, 3.
[8] See Romans 12:6-8, 1 Corinthians 12:1-11, 14:1-2.

raise my hands and tell the whole world, "I love God. I know Jesus. He gave me his spirit." That hour of praying and singing seemed to go by very quickly. Then one of the nuns said, "Let's celebrate Fr. Leo's renewal in the spirit!" So we went and had lemonade and cookies. I sat there and ate the cookies and visited with the others, making small talk the way one does, but Jesus was still right there with me. I couldn't see him but I knew he was there. I wanted to talk to him, but all these people were talking to me too, so I said, "I'll be right back, Lord." But all I really wanted right then was to be alone with the Lord.

Eventually everyone began to drift off to their rooms for the night so I got up and went to the Chapel. There were a couple of people there, but they left almost immediately, so I was alone in the dark with only the candles burning. Never in my life did I pray the way I prayed that night. I was thanking God for everything I never thanked him for before. I don't know if I ever thought of saying, "Thank you, Lord, for my mother. Thank you for my father" and then I was naming my brothers and sisters one by one. Thank you for him and thank you for her, and naming them. Thank you for every teacher I ever had and naming them one by one, and thank you for the priests I knew and I named them one by one. Thank you for this, thank you for that and, Lord, I want to praise you with all the stars that are up in the sky right now, and I praise you with the moon. This just poured out of me and I wanted to stay there all night doing this. The thoughts and words flooded into my mind and heart and just kept pouring and pouring out. Then, suddenly, a strange sound started coming out of my mouth, bubbling out of my mouth. And, I thought, oops, and I put my hand over my mouth and I wondered, "What was that?" Then I realized I must be praying in tongues. But as soon as this thought entered my consciousness I rejected it. "No, no, no, no, no," I thought, "I'm just getting too emotional here and I'm letting my imagination run away with me." I tried to stop but I couldn't. It was like something wanting to bubble out of my mouth that I could not control even when I tried to. I wanted to praise God, but I couldn't find any more words. It was like the Holy Spirit was helping me and all these words are bubbling out of my mouth and I wanted to sing and speak these sounds and to say to God, "I love you, I love you, I love you!"

Finally I left the Chapel and went to bed. In the middle of the night I woke up and this time I heard a sound like a voice singing, not in words but strange sounds. Immediately it came to me, "Oh, Sister Mary is praying in tongues." And then I went right back to sleep. The next morning while we were at breakfast Sr. Mary walked by and I called her over. I said, "You're going to pray in tongues tonight." She looked at me and said, "Thank you" and she walked away with no more reaction than if I had said "I think it's going to rain today."

That night we went to the prayer meeting at Rice High School and when it was all over and we were walking out, I said, "Sr. Mary, you sang in tongues tonight, didn't you?" And she said, "Yes, this was the first time. But how did you know I would?" I said, "Sr. Mary, I don't know if you're going to believe this. I don't know myself what's happening but, in the middle of the night I heard somebody singing in tongues and I knew it was you. I knew you were going to pray in tongues for the first time." "Oh," she said laughing, "You're too much!"

That was Wednesday and it must have been the next day that I got on the bus to go back to Massachusetts. It was a long trip, what with all the stops we made, to get back to my hometown. I sat on the bus and all I wanted to do was praise God. So I sat at the window in the bus looking out and we'd drive by a hill or mountain and I'd say, "Lord, I praise you with that hill or that mountain, with every tree on that mountain, with every leaf on every tree on that mountain and every pine needle, I praise you. I praise you with every blade of grass out there, every flower and every plant. I praise you with that bird flying by and all the songs of the birds." We'd go by a river and I'd say, "Praise you, Lord, with that river and every drop of water that ever went through that river." All this in silence, of course. And then I thought to myself, "I don't know if I'm going to get tired of doing this, but if I get tired, I want every turn of every wheel of this bus to be, 'I love you, I love you, I love you.' As they go around, for all the times that I never told you, I want every wheel on every turn to say, 'I love you, I love you, I love you,' as they go around." And I thought, it's a good thing people don't know what I'm thinking because they'd say, this guy's crazy. But I was so happy. I just wanted to love God and praise God with every drop of water, every star, every hill and every flower, every bird and every person.

When I got home I said to my mother and my sister Jeanne who had picked me up from the bus, "Oh, I've got some wonderful things to tell you." And my mother said, "Yeah, you were suppose to be gone for five days and you were gone almost two weeks. Here you are home from Spain, I don't see you all year, and you go off like that." But I said, "Yeah, but Mom, wait till I tell you what happened. You're going to like it."

Then my brother Edgar came in. He looked at me and he said, "What happened to you?" And I said, "Nothing." "Oh no, don't say nothing," he said, "Come on, tell me, what happened?" I said "What are you talking about?" He said, "I don't know. All I know is that you have something in your face right now that you never had before. I don't know what it is. I don't know if it's joy, if it's light. I don't know. All I know is the day you were ordained a priest and said your first Mass, you didn't look like that. So come on, what happened?" And I said, "Well, yes, something happened, but I don't want to tell you right now. I want to see the whole family together and then I'll tell everybody." He agreed to wait.

TELLING MY FAMILY

So I called all the family who were around town, and asked them if they could come over that night. I don't know how many were there, but there were quite a few. After they all sat down, all looking very curious about why I had invited them to come, I said, "I have something wonderful to tell you." I then told them everything that had happened in Burlington—about how hesitant I was about the whole thing when I first got there, how I finally got convinced, and that I was "prayed with." I decided not to tell them anything about hearing voices in the night or seeing Mary in a kind of a dream because I thought that was just too much to take in and, more importantly, I was afraid of how they might react. I told them the people in Burlington prayed over me and that I felt like a new life had been given to me. I told them I felt so much love for God and I wanted to praise God all the time. I said, "I realize now, as I never have before, that praising God is really the greatest thing we can do, because that's all we're going to do in heaven—so why wait, why not start here!"

Then I asked, "Do you think we could get together as a family, maybe once a week, and just do this together, praise God out loud? I'll show you how to do it. It's not hard." I thought maybe they'd say, "Oh no, we don't want to do that," but instead most were enthusiastic. Some suggested that our cousins and others would probably like to come, too. And one said, "Well, I think some of my children might like to come." And another one said, "I have friends of mine, neighbors—I think they'd like something like that. Can we invite these people?" I said, "You can invite all the people you want. The more the better."

Then someone said, "Where are we going to do this, because you can't do it here in Mom's parlor." So, I said, "You get the people. I'll get the place." So I did. I went to the convent and asked the nuns if they had a room, a hall or something that we could use and they said we could use their basement, a rather big room with a lot of chairs. When I told them why we wanted to use it a couple of nuns said, "Can we go?" "Well, yes, everybody's welcome." So we started doing that, getting together once a week while I was home that summer. That was in 1974 and as far as I know, that prayer group is still going. Not as many people, of course, but they still meet and I think they still meet in the same place.

Over the years the members of this group have said the same thing to me many times—something I want to emphasize to all priests, all Christians; "If only we knew that we *all* have the Holy Spirit. If only we could open our hearts to that. The gifts of the Spirit are for *everybody*. And it should not be something abnormal. It should be something normal for a Christian to live a life of the Spirit and that the gifts of the Spirit would be shown now and then."

RECEIVING GIFTS OF THE SPIRIT

Even as a priest I did not realize receiving gifts of the Spirit in the way I have described—and will describe in more detail later on—was possible. I knew that the great saints did wonderful things; but I thought only the great saints could do those things. Now I realize that it can be part of a normal Christian life. The Holy Spirit can be in you, and when it's necessary—for the good of the community or someone, the Holy Spirit can assist you in different situations. It took me a while to understand this, partly because of my own resistance which I described earlier. I'll give two examples that happened shortly after my experiences in Burlington.

Two or three days after I got home I took some of my nieces and nephews to Mount Monadnock, in Jaffrey, New Hampshire not too far from our hometown in Massachusetts. It's a nice mountain to climb with many trails and its summit is above the timber line, so the views are spectacular in all directions. So many wanted to go I needed help, so one of my brothers came along. We had about fifteen to seventeen children and the two of us driving. When we arrived at the trailhead and parked the cars the kids were already starting to run up the trail. I said, "Wait a minute, come back here, come back here. We're going to say a prayer before we go."

So they all gathered round and I said, "Lord, thank you for this beautiful day and thank you for these beautiful children. We love them. Please watch over them as we go up the mountain. Keep us safe from all harm until we're back home again." And I said, "Thank you," again. Then I said, "Okay, let's go!" After we got above the tree line where it's mostly all rock, dark clouds suddenly came over us and it began to rain. Some of the children became frightened so I called them over to me. This is where I found out about one of the gifts of the spirit, the gift of faith. The *gift* of faith is not the same as the *virtue* of faith. It's a gift that comes now and then on special occasions. I didn't know anything about it until that moment. But all of a sudden I knew what was going to happen. So I said, "Come over here." I said, "Sit down." They said, "It's raining." I said, "I know, but sit down."

So they sat down and I lifted up my arms and hands and I said, "Lord, thank you. We're having so much fun and we thank you. We thank you for this beautiful mountain. Thank you for the rain and thank you for all the fun we're going to have going all the way to the top and coming back. And, thank you for stopping the rain." It did stop, right then and there. And all the kids said, "It stopped, it stopped." And I said, "Of course, it stopped." I said, "Jesus said, 'Ask and you will receive.' Don't be afraid to ask because my Father only gives good things so, you see when you pray, God listens." They were pretty amazed.

We made it all the way to the top and then back down the mountain to the parking area. As soon as we got into the vehicles and closed the doors, the rain started again. And it continued to rain most of the way home.

After we dropped the kids off at their homes and went home ourselves, one of my sisters called me and said, "What in the world did you do?" I said, "What are you talking about?" She said, "My little kids were telling me, 'Mommy, you know what? It was raining and Uncle Leo said a prayer and it stopped.'" I said, "Yea, what's so surprising about that? We're supposed to pray, aren't we?" Well, that's when I realized what the *gift* of faith is. As believers in God we have faith all the time, even though we may waver on the particulars from time to time. The gift of faith, on the other hand, is for special occasions and when it comes, you just know. When I prayed for the rain to stop I knew it would; I had no doubts. But that had never happened to me in my life. Although I had prayed many times for something, I never had had the experience of knowing it was going to happen *right then*. This is how I came to understand the gift of faith.

Another time at a prayer meeting in the sisters' basement we were praying and I gave them songbooks and taught them a few songs and showed them how not to be afraid to pray out loud if you want to praise God and thank God. We praised God with everything—with the stars, the angels and the flowers. We had been praying this way for quite a while when, all of a sudden I knew the Lord wanted to heal somebody. I just knew that God wanted to heal somebody. I got up and I said, "The Lord is really happy with all our prayers here tonight and praising him and he is willing to heal anyone. Does anyone need to be healed of anything?" Nobody moved. So I looked around the room. I couldn't believe that no one wanted to be healed of something. So many of us have aches and pains and different things, but nobody was moving. Then I saw my brother poking his daughter, Karen. "Karen," he said, "You, you." She was hesitating. She was about 16 or 17. So I said, "What is it?" He said, "Well, she has a bad knee. She hurt her knee and she loves to run and jump and was hoping to even teach gymnastics someday. But now she can't do that because her knee hurts. She's seen a couple of doctors and they have not been able to help her." So I invited Karen to sit down on a chair in the middle of the room and told her that she didn't have to do anything.

So Karen sat there and I said to her father, "You come over here with me and we'll put our hands on her and the rest of you just thank God for what He's going to do here, what He *is* doing." I prayed, "Scripture tells us, 'If you believe in

Jesus, lay your hands on the sick and they will be healed.[9] So that's what we're going to do." We put our hands on Karen and I said something like, "Lord, thank you for what you're doing for Karen and for healing her knee, and thank you for everything else tonight." A few minutes went by and then I said, "Okay, Karen, you can go back to your place." We finished the prayer meeting and went home.

The next day, I was sitting in my mother's parlor and all at once the door burst open and in runs Karen screaming, "Uncle Leo, Uncle Leo! My knee, my knee, it's all better. I can run. I can jump. It doesn't hurt anymore. It's all better." And, I said, "I'm not surprised. I kind of knew last night that the Lord wanted to heal someone. It just happened to be you."

Once again, I learned a great deal from this experience, and I was beginning to realize this was part of that new life, the life you live when you live in the Spirit. If we believe what we are told in scripture, especially in the Acts of the Apostles and in some of St. Paul's letters, this should be normal and quite ordinary for Christians. But unfortunately, for most Christians it is not normal.

RETURN TO SPAIN

When I returned to Spain at the end of the summer I didn't tell too many people about my experience in the States right away. I started to look for people who might understand; people I could talk to about this. But there didn't seem to be anyone around who would understand. One of the first things I remember about returning to Spain is that one day after I had finished Mass somebody came up to me and said, "You know, you don't talk the way you used to." I asked what he meant and he said, "Well, the way you said Mass and the way you were speaking at Mass made me think you really believe in

---

[9] James 5:14. See also Mark 6:5, 8:23; Luke 4:40, 13:13; Acts 28:8; Hebrews 6:2.

that." And I said, "Oh yes." And he said, "Well, it is very evident that you believe it!" "You know," he continued, "sometimes I go to Mass and the priest talks and I'm thinking, 'I wonder if he believes this himself.' But I was listening to you today and I said, 'Boy this guy really believes this.'"

This began to happen fairly often that autumn back in Spain. Of course, I was glad about what had happened and I was pleased it showed so that perhaps my belief might touch someone and help them. But I also realized it's not me. This is so important to emphasize—this is the work of God and not me. "You are my God, I thank you." If we have the Holy Spirit within us, which is the spirit of God, we then have the love of God poured into our hearts. If we have all that, then shouldn't we expect beautiful things to happen? I really think God works through us many times and we don't even have the eyes to see it. And sometimes I think we just don't allow him to work through us because of our hesitancy—our unbelief. In any case, things started to happen.

I went back to see the Jesuit priest I knew and I reminded him about the priest from Australia and how he had come to talk about Charismatic Renewal. Then I shared a little bit with him about what had happened during the summer. This is when we agreed to start a group right there. In no time at all that group went from about 12 people to 50 people and then to 100 people, and to 200 people. Wonderful things were happening for so many people, especially young people who were being touched and coming back to their faith and really *living* it.

After two or three years, I began to take these young people on busses for weekends to different parts of Spain where they would tell others about their experiences and I would tell mine. In this way we started prayer groups in Zaragoza, Barcelona, and Bilbao. We were going all over the place and everybody was so impressed by these young people and how they were speaking about Jesus Christ. As this was happening I began to notice all these gifts that I had never thought of before and how the Lord had really given me these gifts.

At one of these retreats that we had gone to give in one city, one particular man came to confession and told me his story. When he finished, I said, "What happened to you when you were just a young boy?" And he looked at me and said, "What do you mean?" I was thinking, "You had a nice new suit on and you were around 7 years old," because I knew that without his telling me. He said to me, "Do you mean when I made my First Communion?" I said, "Yes, that's when it was. You were dressed in a nice new suit and you were around 7 years old." Then I said, "But something happened. What was it?" "Well," he said, "I went to make my first confession and the priest started accusing me of things. He said, 'you must have done this, you must have done that.' And I said, 'No I didn't do that!' And he kept after me and I started crying. Ever since then I've had the hardest time coming to confession." "Yes, I know," I replied. He asked me how I knew that and I said, "I don't know, but the Lord just told me you had a problem and it started when you were 7 years old and now we know it was at your First Communion. Listen. The Lord wants you to know that he loves you and that you have to forgive that priest, if you can. Please try to forgive him. He made a mistake. He was rough. Try to forgive him and you won't be afraid anymore. You'll be free." He seemed so relieved and he said "Oh, thank you so much. Wow! I feel so much better!" I was amazed by this because it was the first time that had ever happened to me. Somehow I was aware that this whole episode was a gift from the Spirit and it awed me and, to tell the truth, scared me a little.

Another time in Bilbao where I had gone to give a retreat a woman stopped me and said, "Oh, Father, please, would you say a prayer for me?" I answered her, "Well, you know they're waiting for me to start Mass." She said, "Please, just a quick prayer." So I said, "Well, okay" and I began by putting my hand on her head and praying in silence. Suddenly I said, "You're afraid of the water, aren't you?" "Oh, yes," she said, "I'm so afraid to get in the water. I'm afraid I'm going to drown." "The Lord doesn't want you to be afraid," I said, "By the way, you do go to the beach too much." She questioned, "How did you know that? I love to go to the beach to get a tan. I spend hours at the beach." I told her, "It's okay to go to the beach, but the Lord really doesn't want you to be so interested in being at the beach and getting a tan. It's not that important, okay?" She said I was right and thanked me. How did I know all that? I had never seen this woman before and I don't know if I have ever seen here since. I just knew.

Another time in Salamanca, one of Spain's major cities, I was asked to pray with the people at the university. As I was praying with the people, a young girl in her late teens I had never seen before asked me to pray with her. I started praying with her but after a short time I stopped and said, "You have a problem with your father, don't you?" She said she did and I asked, "What is it?" But before she could even respond I added, "You don't love your father." She said, "My mother died and less than a year after her death my father married again. I thought that was wrong; he should have waited longer." I said, "Well, I don't know if he should have waited longer or not. All I know is that God wants you to please forgive your father." She looked at me astonished and said, "I don't know if I can." I said, "Well, that is what we have to pray for. Pray with me now and we'll ask God to help you forgive your father." So we prayed together. Later she said, "Okay. I think I can forgive him now." I saw that girl a year or two later and she told me that she was getting married and asked me if I could do the wedding because she said that from that day when she was able to forgive her father her life had changed.

Another time I went to Madrid and a priest asked me to go with him to see a couple he knew that had some sort of problem. So we went to visit them and sat in their parlor together. The woman's name was Paloma and they were explaining to me that she didn't sleep very well at night. She would get nightmares every single night and sleep so poorly that when she got up in the morning she would feel worse than when she had gone to bed.

They asked if I would pray about that. But before I did I told the woman that I wanted to ask her a few questions. When people tell me things like this I like to ask and get an idea of who these people are and what might have happened to precipitate their problem. I try not to be too direct about my questions. So I asked her what she remembered about her childhood. She said that when she was born her parents were not married and not long after her birth she was put in an orphanage with some nuns about which she had only good memories. She said the nuns knew of one aunt she had in Cadiz, down in southern Spain. When she was old enough to travel they put her on a train and sent her down to be with her aunt for a few weeks in the summertime. She also said that her aunt was a schoolteacher and never married and was very, very strict.

She said, "I really didn't want to go. I would have preferred staying at the orphanage, because when I got to my aunt's, she treated me so strictly." Then she said, "You won't believe what she did one night. One night she got a call that some relative had died and they wanted her to come and identify the body. She made me go with her even though I was only 8 or 9 years old at the time. At the hospital when we got to the door of the morgue, I said, 'I'll wait here. She said, 'No, you're coming with me.' And she pulled me inside with her. We started walking between these stretchers where I suppose there were dead bodies. We stopped at one body that was covered and they took the sheet off and revealed a dead person. My aunt nervously said, 'Yes that's my relative.' When we came out of the morgue I remember how frightened I was. I thought, 'I'll never forget this. I'll never forgive what she did to me.' And I've never been able to forget that. As a matter of fact, my aunt called me the other night. She's rather elderly now and she fell and broke her hip."

Then Paloma said to me, "You know, Father, I think I was glad to hear she had broken her hip." So I asked her a few more questions and we spoke about a few other things and then I said, "Well, I think I know what to do now. I am going to ask you to close your eyes and make believe that you are 8 years old and I am going to ask you to remember that scene when you went to the hospital with your aunt. Go through the whole thing again, but this time I want you to see Jesus with you. I want Jesus to go with you and you tell me if he says anything or does anything. So she said, "Well, okay" and closed her eyes and waited. I don't know how much time went by but after a while she opened her eyes and said, "I'm sorry. I just can't do this. I can't imagine this." I said, "Okay, then wait a minute. Let's say a prayer. So we prayed and I asked the Lord to help her out. Then I said, "Let's try again. Close your eyes." She closed her eyes and waited, and all of a sudden her face lit up, with her eyes still closed, she said, "Yes, yes, now I see Jesus and he's coming with us. We're getting on a train. He's with us and we're going into the city and we're getting off the train and he's coming with us. He's coming into the hospital. We get to the door of the morgue and Jesus tells me to go in with my aunt because, he says, she is more afraid than I am." Then she said, "I didn't know she was more afraid than I was! But she was afraid even though she was a grown-up and I was only 8 years old." Then she continued, "We go in and Jesus is with us and we go to see the body. Then we come out and the door closes and Jesus says, 'Thank you. Your aunt needed you to be with her because she was so afraid.' And then he's gone." She opened her eyes and said. "I didn't know she was more afraid than I was. I was just a little girl. Father, would you do me a favor?" "Of course," I said, "What is it?" And she said, "Could we pray for my aunt for her hip to be healed?" And as soon as she asked that question I knew she was going to be okay. And so we did; we said a prayer for her aunt. I didn't see this woman again for another year. When I did see her, she and her husband told me that since the night of my visit; she had been sleeping very, very well. No more problems, no more nightmares, just sleeping so well. So that was another case where I realized how great Jesus Christ is and how he had come into my life in a new way and that I had all these graces and gifts that he was offering to others through me by the power of the Holy Spirit. I began to use these gifts more consciously and deliberately and I saw many beautiful things happening.

GROWING IN THE SPIRIT

By now I was living in Valladolid. It is a rather big city where there is a Scots College and an English College. These schools were given to the English and Scots Catholic Church during the persecution in England so they could train priests who would later go back to England. A lot of these priests were martyred and some are beatified or canonized saints now. One day the rector of the Scots College asked me if I would come and speak to his students. They were all in philosophy and theology classes and getting ready to be ordained priests. He said to me, "I don't know anything about Charismatic Renewal but I think it is something they should know about. Would you speak to us about that?"

So I went one night and I gave a talk to all the students and the faculty. I told them about the renewal movement and I explained my own experience. I said how, in spite of being a priest and a religious, I had not *really* known Jesus Christ until that day in Burlington when they prayed over me and the Holy Spirit came to me in a special way when all of a sudden I knew Jesus Christ in a new way and in a way that I couldn't doubt anymore. I told them that from that time on my faith wasn't just in my head; it was in my heart. When my talk finished I said a prayer for everybody asking God to bless them all and for the Holy Spirit to fill them too.

The next day the Rector of the Scots College came over and we sat in my office and he just looked at me. He was almost in tears and he said, "Please, help me." I said, "What's the matter?" And he said, "I've got to make a confession to you. Last night, after you left, I told the other priests that were with me that you ought to be ashamed of yourself, coming here and telling us and all these seminarians that you didn't know Jesus Christ even though you had been a priest for 19 years. He continued, "I went to bed and the next morning I got up and felt rather strange; I couldn't figure out how I felt. But you know? I smoke and I've always wanted to stop but I couldn't. But I was going downtown and walking down the street and I just took my cigarettes and threw them away. I'm not smoking anymore. I went by a church and I said to myself, 'I've got to go in here,' and I just knelt and I couldn't stop praying. And I just felt so full of, I don't know what—peace, joy, faith, hope, love. I don't know what it is but all I know is that something happened to me. Please can you explain what happened to me and help me out?" He continued to say, "Now I think I know what you were talking about last night and I'm starting to think something is happening to me."

I said, "Well, we did say a prayer together last night and I asked the Holy Spirit to come. I guess that's what happened—I guess he did!" This was not surprising to me. This priest joined our prayer group after that and became very enthusiastic about the whole thing and really a blessing to the whole prayer group with his own prayer life and his own testimony.

One night while I was in Rome in 1977, Sister Briege McKenna, an internationally renowned speaker on healing, who was healed herself of very serious arthritis through charismatic prayer, was giving a talk so I mentioned it at my House and I asked the Superior if he wanted to go with me.[10]

There must have been at least 100 priests there. There were bishops and I know Leo Jozef Cardinal Suenens was there from Belgium.[11] Sister Briege told of her experience of healing and talked about Jesus Christ and how the Holy Spirit worked in her life. At the end she said, "And now if you don't mind I would like to say a prayer for all of you." So everybody knelt down. And she said, "Oh no, you can sit." But we all wanted to kneel. So we knelt down and she said this beautiful prayer out loud asking God to bless us all and fill us with his Holy Spirit and for Jesus Christ to be Lord of all things and of each of us.

As the Superior and I got on the bus to go home I said to him, "You better get ready." And he said, "What do you mean?" And I said, "Well, this nun is pretty powerful with her praying and she prayed over all of us, and if you were the least bit open to what she was praying about, the Holy Spirit might just touch you and you might realize that he has and you just might see a change in your life. I'm just telling you that it's possible." He sloughed this off saying, "I don't know what you're talking about."

The next day one of the other priests asked me if I'd go to a movie at an English theater with him. We arrived home rather late, and, as we came up the stairs the Superior came out of his room and called to me and said, "Please come into my room." He closed the door and said, almost in tears: "Please

[10] Briege McKenna, Henry Libersat, *Miracles Do Happen: God Can do the Impossible.* Servant Books / St. Anthony Messenger Press, 1987.
[11] Cardinal Suenens, Archbishop of Mechelen, Belgium, was a vocal leader at the Second Vatican Council and an advocate of reform in the Catholic Church. He died in 1996.

help me." I said, "What's wrong?" He said, "I don't know. All I know is I was sitting here with my Bible in my hands thinking about a cousin who had written to me about a problem, and what could I say, and all of sudden something like a voice told me to look in the Bible. The voice told me what chapter and what verse to look for. It turned out to really be the answer to my cousin's problem. Odd, but I just feel so full of something, like I'm going to burst. I don't know what it is—peace, joy, love, hope, and faith? I don't know. All I know is I want to pray and I feel so happy." I said, "Well I told you last night that something might happen and I think that all that happened is that the Holy Spirit has touched you. That's all." He seemed incredulous so I said, "C'mon, let's say a prayer together now." So we said a prayer and I left him.

The following week, a nun at a convent where we La Salette priests took turns saying Mass said, "What happened to Father Superior?" I said, "I don't know, why do you ask?" She said, "Well, last week when he came every day to say Mass, his face was just so lit up and he was grinning all through the Mass with a big smile on his face. He was so happy." I said, "Well, maybe something happened. Why don't you ask him?"

Things like this were happening all around me by now, I wasn't too surprised at this. One day I was in our chapel in Valladolid and I had my Bible opened to Philippians 4:13, where Paul says, "I have the strength for everything through him who empowers me." All of a sudden, I'm not sure why or how, I felt compelled to tell someone about this message from Philippians. I knew who the somebody was: a girl used to be in our prayer group who had gone back to her village to take care of her mother and father who were sick. The next day I had to go to Madrid so I took a detour and I went to her village. I walked into her house and she said, "What are you doing here?" I said, "I've got to tell you something. The Lord wants you to look at Philippians Chapter 4, verse 13." So she opened her Bible and looked up the verse and she started to cry.[12] She said through her tears, "I've been having such a hard time here trying to take care of my mother and father and, do you know that's my favorite line in the Bible?" I said, "Last night I was praying in the chapel, and I felt the Lord wanted me to come tell you that. He wants to remind you of that. You can do all things in him who strengthens you. So here I am sharing this with you. That's all I'm here for." She was overjoyed. I got back in my car and drove to Madrid. I don't know how but I was so sure I had to go there and tell her that and it was exactly what she needed to hear.

SISTER LUISA BERTANI

While in Rome I received a letter from a friend whom I had met in Spain at the American air base who was now back in Louisiana with her husband. She told me there were some nuns from Italy at her Louisiana parish. One of the nuns, much beloved for her goodness, had suddenly returned home to Italy because she was dying of cancer. She was a good friend to this woman and so she asked me if I would visit her in Rome. She gave me the address of the convent which I easily found on my map of Rome. On the 8th of December, 1977— easy to remember because it was the Feast of the Immaculate Conception of Mary—I got on the bus. When I got to the street where she lived and found the convent, I went up and rang the bell. A sister opened the door who greeted me in Italian. In my broken Italian I was able to say, "I would like to see Sr. Luisa Bertani. She looked at me sadly and said, "She died." I said as well as I could in Italian, "I don't speak Italian. I speak English." "*Aspetta*," which means, "Wait a moment." She soon came back with another nun who spoke English who asked, "Can I help you?" I told her I had come to see Sr. Luisa.

---

[12] "I have the strength for everything through him who empowers me."

"Well, come in and sit down. As sister probably told you, she died a few days ago." I said, "Yes, I understood that." She said, "Well, did you know her?" I said, "No, I didn't know her but a friend of mine in the United States knew her and said that she was very good and asked would I stop by to see her." She replied, "Yes, she was very good. In fact, I think she was a saint—*is* a saint."

She added, "She was my best friend. When she was dying, I was with her. I said to her, 'Luisa, when you get to heaven, will you send us roses, the way St. Theresa said she would do? St. Theresa in France said she would send roses.' She opened her eyes and she said to me, 'No, I will send you carnations.' She closed her eyes then. She was in a lot of pain, and finally I dared to say, 'Luisa, why carnations instead of roses?' And she opened her eyes and said, 'Because roses, when they fade lose their petals; but carnations, when they fade, don't lose their petals, they stay together, and I want to pray in heaven that all of you in the community, in all families and communities, you stay together, that you love each other; so I'll send you carnations.' That was the last thing she said before she died."

I decided it was time to leave so I thanked her and said goodbye. I went home and I wrote my friend a letter saying her dear friend had died and related the story that I was told about Sister Luisa and the carnations.

Sometime much later I got a letter from my friend in Louisiana and she wrote, "I took your letter to my parish. When I got there a prayer group was going on and I knew that they knew Sister Luisa, so I read them your letter." She continued to write, "Several days later one of the women in the group was looking for a school, a Catholic school for her little boy. She went to one school and they said, 'No, there's no room.' She went to another school and again there was no room. There was only one other school in the area but before she went to this school she prayed, 'Sister Luisa, would you find a Catholic school for my boy?' She then went to the school where they told her they would make room for the boy.

When she got home she kept thinking about how her prayer had seemed to be answered so she prayed again saying 'Sister Luisa, if you're the one who helped me, why don't you send me carnations?' Would you believe that after a little while on that same day, the doorbell rang. At the door there was a young man with a bunch of carnations, and he said, 'Here, these are for you.' I said, 'From whom? And he said, 'There's a little envelope here.' I opened the envelope and it said they were from a friend of mine. So I called my friend and I said, 'Hey, thank you for the carnations.' And she said, 'Carnations? No, no, I sent you some other flowers. That was a mistake.' She said, 'I'm sorry, I wanted you to get...'. I forget what they were. She continued to say, 'I'll call the flower shop and tell them they made a mistake.' She said to her friend, 'No, please don't call, wait till I tell you what happened.'"

So here I have this letter from my friend in the States telling me this beautiful story and I thought, "Isn't that wonderful?" I was always being invited to speak to nuns and so now and then I would tell them this story, and I believe I told my prayer group in Spain this story too, because I was telling everybody who would listen about this.

One day I had gone to the convent of the Sisters of St. Theresa, and I told the nuns this story. A few weeks later I was going by the convent and I stopped by. When I got inside this nun said, "Oh Father, I was hoping to see you. Come here, I've got to tell you something." We sat down and she said, "Do you remember when you came here last time and you told us the story about Sister Luisa Bertani, and how she said she would send carnations? Well, my nephew went down to Madrid to look for a job and he asked me to pray for him so that he could find a job and a place to live, you know, an apartment or something that wouldn't cost too much. He was staying in some kind of a *penzione* and it was costing him a little money and he called me once or twice and said, 'please keep praying for me, I still don't have a job and I still don't have a place.' I said, 'I will, I'm praying.' So, after you told us that story I said, 'I know, I'll pray to Sister Luisa.' So I asked Sister Luisa,

'Would you help my nephew find a job and a place to stay?' Well, she continued, "A day or two later I got a call from my nephew and he said, 'Auntie, I got a job and I got a place to stay, so thank you for your prayers.' I said, 'That's great. You're welcome.' She hung up and a little while later the doorbell rang. She said, "I went to the door and there's a man with a bunch of carnations, and he said, 'I was just going by and I had these carnations, and I thought maybe you could put them on your altar here in the convent.' 'Imagine that, Luisa sent us carnations!'"

Another woman, Pilar, who was a secretary at the American air base in Spain told me she had prayed to Sister Luisa for her father who was having some kind of trouble. After she had been praying at her desk, she had gone out of her office on an errand for her boss who was the Chaplain at the air base. When she came back she found that somebody— she had no idea who—had put a carnation on her desk. So I often encourage people to pray to Sister Luisa Bertani, a person who was touched deeply by the Holy Spirit and has brought healing to many people.

HOLY SISTERS

As I said earlier I was taught by nuns before entering the seminary. And through the years I have met many wonderful and holy sisters in Christ who have shared their experiences with me. Over the years I had many opportunities to visit convents and offer retreats and talks and to minister to sisters in my capacity as a priest.

One time while I was living in Spain I met the cloistered nuns in Olmedo, near Valladolid. I had given them a talk and when they heard that I spoke English and French, they said, "You know we have founded convents in different parts of the world and one of our convents is on an island in Greece, a small island. There are very few Catholics and there is only one priest there, and all he speaks is Greek and French.

You speak Spanish and English and French. Those poor nuns are all by themselves out there. Could you perhaps go there and give them a retreat or something?" "Go to Greece?" I said, hesitatingly. They quickly added, "We'll pay for your trip." "Oh well," I said, laughing, "now it's getting hard to refuse." A short time later I flew to Athens and took another plane from Athens to Santorini, the southernmost island from Athens before you get to Crete. And as soon as I got there I went to the convent to see all the nuns. Almost all of them spoke Spanish. There were two nuns who had been there with the original group, one of whom was in her nineties. She was Italian. The other one was Greek but she spoke Italian. I stayed there for a month giving them many talks on prayer and the gifts of the Holy Spirit.

One day the Superior said to me, "Our old Italian nun is very sick and I'm afraid she may die. Would you come in and give her the Sacraments? It's a cloistered convent but we have permission, in a case like this, to open the doors and let you in." She said that at a certain time in the afternoon they would open the door to the cloister for me. So I went to my room and all of a sudden I felt compelled to open my Bible. I opened it and I found some words that left me with the feeling that I had to tell them to the sick nun. She was Italian and I can read Italian so I went to the Superior and asked her for an Italian Bible.

When it was time, I walked into the sister's room with the Italian Bible. She was very sick and frail. In my broken Italian I was able to tell her that I was going to read something from the Bible. So I began to read a certain passage. When I finished she was in tears and she said, "Father, years ago, when I was in Italy, during the war, I was put in a prison with some other nuns. It looked very bad for us at one time. I opened my Bible and these were the same words that appeared. Where the Lord says in Isaiah, 'Do not fear, for I am with you, do not be afraid, for I am your God; I will strengthen you, I will help you, I will uphold you with my victorious right hand."[13] And she said, "One other time after that something had happened and those same words came to me, and here I am ninety two years old and you come to me with these same words." I said, "God told me to read this to you. 'Don't be afraid; I'm with you.'" She was overjoyed.

Things like this had never happened before my friends in Burlington prayed over me that the Holy Spirit would come to me and renew me. Before I opened my heart to the Holy Spirit and realized I could be a vehicle for all this power I was counting on my own power instead of the power of God. And that's all it is really.

Another time I went to a summer retreat place to give a week-long retreat to a group of teaching nuns. One day one of the nuns came and asked if she could speak to me about something. She said, "It's kind of embarrassing, but I have nobody to talk to." She continued, "One Friday night I was in chapel praying. All of sudden I fell on the floor. That never happened to me before. I don't know how long I stayed down there, but when I got up I had an awful pain in my side." She went on, "I went up to my room to get ready for bed, and when I took my clothes off I saw I had a wound in my side that was bleeding. Every Friday it bleeds and it hurts terribly. I haven't been able to tell anybody this. I want to know what you think."

This took me a bit off guard, so, I said, "Sister, let me think about this and I'll talk to you again in a couple of days, okay?" Since these nuns were not cloistered I was able to see them more and I was even able to eat in the dining room with them. So for the next couple of days I surreptitiously tried to keep my eye on this particular nun. I soon realized that she was always smiling, always happy, and she was always helping all the other nuns, especially the older nuns. Some of them were very old and she would always help them sit down and get up and clean their plates and things like that. And after everybody

---

[13] Isaiah 41:10.

was done she would be the one who stayed and cleaned up the dining room, always smiling. And I thought, "These are very good signs. She seems so normal. And she's happy and she is loving."

A few days after our first conversation she came to see me again and I said, "Sister, are you able to do what you have to do, like teach and all the other work you have to do?" She said, "Yes, the bleeding is just on Fridays and it does not stop me from doing the things that I have to do." So I told her, "I asked you this because if ever you can't do what you have to do, then you have to say to God, 'I don't want this. I can't have this because I have to do my duty. My duty comes first.' But since you *can* do your duty, whether it's teaching or other work, I think this could be a grace from God who is asking you to suffer with Jesus, especially on Fridays, for the salvation of others. Would you be willing to do that?" "Oh yes," she said. "You're willing to suffer a little more on Fridays with Jesus for the salvation of other people?" She said, "Yes." I said, "What else can I tell you Sister? This is a grace from God. Just thank God and offer it to God. Offer it for the salvation of others. I think that's what all of this is."[14] And I do really believe that this is true. I felt so privileged to have met her and to know there are people like this in our midst.

Then another time I was asked to be spiritual director for a novice in a cloistered convent where I used to give talks. When we met in the convent parlor the novice would be behind bars that separated us. One day when I was speaking with her I said, "When I come to give talks to the community I notice that there's something special about one of the sisters. I don't know what it is, but there's something in her face that's special." The novice asked, "Which one is it?" And I said, "She always sits on the right, always the same place." She looked at me and she said, "Yes, Father, I think she's special too." She added, "I'm going to tell you something but don't let her know

---

[14] See *Catechism of the Catholic Church*, ¶1508 and ¶1521. For a biblical warrant, see 2 Corinthians 12:9 and Colossians 1:24.

I told you. She doesn't know I know, but one day I came in chapel and was walking down the aisle and she was kneeling down in front. When I got near the front, I noticed that she was about a foot or two off the floor. She wasn't even touching the floor. She was on her knees, but she wasn't even touching the floor. And she was all wrapped in prayer. So, I just turned around and I walked out. I never told her I saw her. So, I think she *is* special."

I hear from that nun about once a year. She usually sends me a note just to tell me that she's praying for me. I feel so privileged to know that all these things are happening with so many holy sisters who have devoted their lives to prayer. Their example shows us what is available to anyone. They are special in and of themselves, just as we are all special to God. But they are also special because they have chosen to give themselves so completely to Christ.

THE GYPSY NUN

One day I went by bus with a group from Spain to the La Salette Shrine in France and to the mountain where Our Lady appeared. In the part of the hotel where I was staying, I was close to a lot of French people and I noticed that there was a young nun with them. When she came by me and said, "Hello," I thought there was something about her face that was exceptional. She looked so young, but I knew there was something else special about her; I didn't know what it was.

Later on we went to the dining room for supper and all the Spanish people were sitting together and I looked over and saw the group of French people including the young nun. And again, I thought, "There's something special about her face, and how she prayed so piously." And then later that evening I saw her in the Basilica sitting by herself in the corner with her eyes closed and her hands on her lap, so deep into prayer and I thought, "Gosh, I wonder who she is. There is definitely something special about her, and I thought, she doesn't look French. She's with all these French people and she's speaking French, but she doesn't look French." I noticed her like that again the next day, and then again on Saturday.

On Sunday morning I said to the Spanish group, "If you would like to come down to where Our Lady appeared, there's a fountain of water flowing there, and anybody who's not feeling well may want to drink some of the water. And we'll say prayers for you to be well." So we went down, some drank the water, and I began a prayer with them, one by one, so they'd be well. And I noticed on the hill right next to me, this same nun was sitting by herself with her eyes closed, praying.

The Basilica of Our Lady of La Salette in the French Alps

I was there quite a while, praying one by one with all these people. When I finished I walked up the steps where Our Lady had gone and I began to walk toward the Basilica. Then, for some reason, I turned around and looked back and that nun was coming toward me. I was so curious about her and drawn to her holiness that I just felt I had to talk to her. I waited for her to catch up with me and I said, "Excuse me, Sister, what community do you belong to?" So she looked at me with a sweet look and said with a sweet voice, "I'm a Sister of Compassion." Then she asked me, "What were you doing down there? Were you praying with the sick people?" I said, "Yes, Sister, you know, just a few years ago somebody said to me, 'If you believe in Jesus and the power of the Holy Spirit why aren't you praying for sick people to be healed?' Jesus said we should do that." I said, "I didn't used to do that but I started doing it and people started to be healed." And she looked at me and said, "Oh yes, of course, it's the word of God, isn't it?" "Oh, yes, Sister, isn't it beautiful?" And she said, "Oh, I know." Then I said, "This is all still kind of new to me and I know I'm learning a lot. Can we just sit down here and talk for a few minutes?"

So we sat down on a little wall there and people were walking by and I started telling her about some of the things I had learned in the Bible and she was listening and all of a sudden she said to me, "Oh, I'm going to tell my people about that." I wondered what she meant by "my people." I kept on talking and I told her something else that I learned from the Bible and again she said, "Oh I'm going to tell my people that too." So I said, "Sister, excuse me, but what do you mean 'your people?'" She answered, "I am a gypsy."

I was floored when she said that because in Spain there were a lot of gypsies and they all have a bad reputation for stealing and cheating. I guess I looked surprised because she then said, "You see, I lived my life in a covered wagon traveling around France with my family. One day when I was 16 years old I broke my nose and I had to go to a hospital. There were some nuns working there in the hospital and they took care of me. I had never seen a nun up close like that. I kept looking at them and I kept thinking, 'I wonder what's special about these women. They've got something in their faces; I wish I knew what it was.' And I kept looking at them and I didn't want to leave because I wanted to know what they had that I didn't have, but I wasn't there very long and I had to leave. All of a sudden I realized what they had that I did not have: they knew God. And I thought, 'Oh, I wish I could know God like that.'" She continued, "I started looking for God; everywhere I went I'd look for God. When we traveled in a covered wagon I'd look out and see if I could find God somewhere. Once when we were camped for the night I walked to the nearest village and I went into the church and I said, 'I think maybe this is God's house. I think maybe this is where you find God.'" She said she looked around and there was nobody there and then she said, "I walked down front and I looked around, still looking for God. Then I saw this big book and I went over to the book, but I had never gone to school and I didn't know how to read or write, but I was able to make out the name of the book, the title on the top of the book said, 'Bible.' Somehow I was aware that this was a book about God. So I opened it up and I was looking for pictures or something to tell me about God but there was only writing and I couldn't understand any of it. So I started to cry because I was with a book that could tell me what I longed to know and I couldn't understand."

She resolved then to go to church on Sundays so she could listen to stories about God. She said, "Every Sunday wherever we camped, I'd walk to the village and go into the church. I'd be sitting on a bench and people would move away from me because they could tell by the way I was dressed that I was a gypsy; they were afraid of me. I didn't know how to act in church, so I'd watch them and when they got up, I got up and when they sat down, I'd sit down and when they knelt, I'd kneel."

She did this for two years, going to church whenever she could and listening to all she could learn about God. After two years, she turned 18 and was supposed to get married, because gypsy girls get married when they reach that age. Her family kept asking her when she was going to get married. She explained, "The way we get married is, we go off with some guy we think is okay and we just leave and go with him. Then we come back and look for our families and we tell them we got married and that's all there is to it."

One night, sitting around the campfire with her family, she told them she did not intend to get married. They were shocked and said, "What do you mean you're not going to get married. You're supposed to get married!" She said, "I'm not going to get married. I want to be a nun." Her sister threatened to kill her if she became a nun and she believed that her sister was very serious about this.

The following Sunday after Mass she got up her courage and followed the priest into the sacristy. When he turned and saw her there she said, "I want to go to confession." She didn't really know what confession was but she had heard over the previous two years that you should go to confession. When the priest agreed to hear her confession she said, "No, no, no, I don't want to go to confession." So he asked her what she *did* want and she replied "I want to know what to do to become a nun." He asked, "What kind of nun?" She answered, "Is there more than one kind?" He said, "Of course. There are cloistered nuns, who don't leave the convent." She didn't think she wanted that, having lived in a covered wagon all her life. "Or," the priest continued, "there are nuns who teach or take care of the sick, and do other good work."

Something like that sounded right to her and she told the priest so. He offered to write to the nuns where his own sister had been a nun before she died to ask them if they would take her.

Weeks went by and the priest had no news for her. She was becoming anxious because spring was coming and she was afraid she would have to leave with her family. Finally the priest visited her father and mother and said, "I would like to take your two girls with me to Besancon (a big city nearby)." He added, "We'll be back tonight."

The nun explained, "He took my sister along because I told him she was going to kill me if I went to a convent. He took the two of us and we went to the convent. The nuns asked me what I wanted so I told my story. They said, 'Oh those nuns you met at the hospital when you broke your nose are our nuns! That's our hospital.' Then I told them, 'I would like to be a nun.' So they said, 'Well, we'll think about it and let you know, maybe you could be a postulant.' 'No,' I said, 'I don't want to be a postulant; I want to be a *nun*.' They said, 'First you have to be a postulant, then you have to be a novice and *then* you become a nun.'"

The sisters told her to go home and told her they would get back to her and let her know their decision. She said that her sister said, after she met the nuns, "Well, they're pretty nice; so we'll wait. I won't kill you right now."

Finally, the letter came that she could enter. When she got there, the Superior or Mistress of Novices assigned a young nun to show her around, show her where her locker was and her bed and so forth and tell her something about the schedule. The young nun said, "Today is Sunday, so this afternoon at 4:00, we have vespers and Benediction of the Blessed Sacrament." So the gypsy girl said, "What is that?" The nun said, "You don't know?" She said, "No, I have no idea." She said, "When the bell rings, you come with me and you'll see." The bell rang and the two of them went into the chapel and took a place and all the nuns came in and they gave her a book and they started singing vespers. And they would show her in the book where the page was, but she couldn't read and was unable to follow.

When vespers were over they started the Benediction of the Blessed Sacrament. The priest came out and put the host inside the monstrance and put it up on the altar, and all the nuns bowed their heads. She said, "I was petrified, and I screamed, 'What are you doing, what are you doing? Why are you putting your heads down? What's in that sun up there?' "She said the monstrance looked to her like the sun with all the rays. They just told her to be quiet. Then the young nun bent over and said, "You see that white in the middle there. That's bread. Well, not really bread. That bread is Jesus Christ. Jesus himself." And this young gypsy nun looked at me when she told me that and she said, "You know, Father, that was easy for me to believe because I already had Jesus in my heart. And I thought if I have him in my heart, why can't he be in that bread?"

Here was a young, unsophisticated gypsy girl who didn't know anything about the faith, about the Catholic Church, and she was able to say, "That's easy to believe. I've already got him in my heart." What an incredible grace from God! As Benediction ended she knew she was going to like life as a nun.

The next day, the Mistress of Novices called her in and said, "Well, Sister, if you want to be a nun you have to learn to pray." And this simple gypsy girl had no idea what this meant. So the Mistress of Novices explained, "Praying is just talking to God and listening to God." And she said, "Oh, Sister, I've been doing that for two years now, ever since that day in the hospital when I started looking for God, I started talking to him. And he talks to me too. That's how I knew I shouldn't get married and that I should be a nun. I know what he's trying to tell me."

She was astonished to learn that what she had been doing so naturally for two years was praying and she realized how much she was going to enjoy the life of a nun. As I took in this amazing story all I could think was that I had been a priest and religious all those years with vows and I was still finding it difficult to pray and she says, "Oh, that's easy. I've been doing that for a couple of years, talking to God, listening to God as he talks to me." After she told me this I said, "But it must have been difficult for you." She said, "Oh yes, it was very difficult. I wasn't used to being in one house like that and not going out much, but the Mistress of Novices was very good to me and she understood my struggles. So she'd call me aside and she'd say, 'You're having a hard time, aren't you?' And when I said I was she would reply, "Pack a lunch and go out anywhere you want and come back this evening. Go out in the fields, if you want, and run around." In her early months at the convent she would often pack a lunch and go out and run all over the fields and get tired out and then come back. This would always make her feel better and she was okay until the next time.

Then I asked her, "Well, how about now?" She said, "Now I'm a nun and I have vows. At first I had to learn to read and write and then I had to make my First Communion and be Confirmed and receive all the Sacraments. Now I have vows and I'm studying the Bible because I want to work with my people, the gypsies. I want to tell them about these things that you've been telling me, too." I said, "Now I know what you mean when you say 'your people.'" She said, "Yes, I want to work with my people and tell them all about God and all about the Bible because other churches and religions come and they tell them things about the Bible and, of course, they believe it, but I want to tell them the truth from the Catholic Church. So that's what I'm going to do." I said, "Well, thank you, Sister, for telling me your story." And she said, "Thank you for what you told me too." I said, "Sister, could we pray?" She said, "Oh, yes." So sitting there on that wall, people walking by, she closed her eyes and she opened her hands out and she said, "Dear Lord, thank you so much for bringing Fr. Leo into my life today. I thank you for that blessing and I ask you, please bless him too." I was almost in tears. I said a prayer and then I said, "Sister, I'm leaving tomorrow to go back to Spain." She said, "Well, I'm leaving too." So I said, "I probably won't see you anymore, but I'll see you in heaven." And she said, "Oh yes, of course." I said, "Oh, but I didn't get your name." She said her name was Miriam and then we said goodbye.

A few years later, I was at our shrine in Attleboro, Massachusetts. As I was going by the desk where people stop by with questions, I heard someone speaking in what sounded like a French accent. I went over and there was a young man there inquiring about the Shrine. "You wouldn't be French, would you?" I asked. He said, "Yes, I am." So we began to speak French. He told me he was from France and working with a company in Taunton for a year. He came over to see the Shrine and wanted to know all about it. So I gave him a walking tour of the Shrine, explaining things as we went along. I told him that La Salette was a French community that started at the Shrine in France. He had heard of the Shrine but did not know much about the apparition, so I told him about it.

He came back once or twice more and as a result, we got to be good friends. During one of his visits I told him about meeting Sister Miriam—the gypsy nun in France and what she had said, which interested him a great deal.

A few months later, after he had returned to France, I got a letter from him and in it was a page from a French magazine. The article was on prayer in France and a whole page was on Sister Miriam. The article related some of the things she had told me. In the article she tells that now she has a motor home—what we would call a recreational vehicle—which she drives around France looking for gypsies. When she finds gypsies, she stops on the side of the road and calls all the children over and they come into her RV. And then she begins to teach them about God, and Jesus, and God's love for them. The article said that the RV was all windows and the parents, especially the mothers, would come over, lean near the RV, and listen to everything Sister Miriam was saying. This pleased me so much because this is what she had said she wanted to do. I always thought that story would make such a beautiful movie—this gypsy living in a covered wagon who after finding God gives her life to bringing the Good News of Jesus Christ to her own people.

HEALINGS

One of the things that amazed me the most about the power of prayer and the Holy Spirit was how many people were healed from all kinds of infirmities when they were prayed over by myself and others whose faith had been deepened by our own powerful experiences of God through prayer. I can't even remember all the people who were healed when I prayed with them, only the more dramatic ones. The experience with my niece, Karen, and her knee was the first one I personally experienced. But there were many more in Spain and in the United States in the summers when I would return for vacation. As you read the accounts that follow, I want to emphasize again how these things came about. Although I may have been involved, it was God's power and God's power alone that healed others of their illnesses. God may have used me as a kind of vehicle for his power, but it was not I, but God, who healed anyone.

I remember once in Barcelona a lady who had a very bad sinus infection asked me to pray with her. She had been to the doctors and they had taken an X-ray which showed that her sinuses were all blocked. I prayed with her and, it didn't take very long; she suddenly felt much, much better. She went back to the doctor and he told her that her sinuses were all cleared up. Now, again, I'm not talking here so much about miracles. I do believe in miracles, but I'm talking here about the power of prayer. It is important to understand what Scripture says (James 5:14-15a): "Is anyone among you sick? He should summon the presbyters of the church, and they should pray over him and anoint (him) with oil in the name of the Lord, and the prayer of faith will save the sick person, and the Lord will raise him up."[15]

At St. Anne's Church in Leominster, I was praying one evening for healing and explaining how the Lord heals. The following week a young woman came to the meeting and said, "I was here last week. I just walked into the church and I heard you talking about how the Lord heals. I had just been in the hospital. I burned my hand and they had wrapped it all up. It was burned real bad." So she continued, "If that's what he thinks, here's my hand, let my hand be healed. You said a prayer for healing. Would you believe? I went home and took the bandage off and there was nothing on my hand. It wasn't red anymore. There was no sign of any burning." She said, "I still have the record from the hospital, what the doctor said about my burn, and how bad it was." She said, "I want you to know, you were right. That the Lord heals."

Another night in that same church, they brought in a woman who had very bad arthritis. She had a lot of trouble moving around and she had to be helped into church in a wheelchair. They brought her right up near the altar and helped her out of the wheelchair and up a couple of steps to me. I laid my hands on her and said a few prayers. Within moments she started to jump up and down. Then she ran up and down the stairs, shouting, "I'm healed, I'm healed." She was actually

---

[15] See also Luke 9:2 and Acts 4:30.

running up and down the stairs yelling, "I'm healed, I'm healed, and my arthritis is gone." I still remember her name. Her name was Louise.

A friend of my mother's, a rather elderly lady, who had a lot of arthritis in her hand and a lot of pain, asked me to pray for her. I prayed and she told me later that her hand straightened out and the pain was all gone.

There was another lady, Mrs. Collette—I can't remember her first name—who was bedridden and having trouble breathing. She needed oxygen to help her breathe and the doctors thought she wouldn't live very long. I went and prayed with her and a short time later she was fine and able to breathe normally. In fact, I saw her more than once in the years that followed that day in the hospital.

I must point out here that people were not always healed in the expected way, or exactly in the way that was requested, but there was always something that happened. I really believe that when you pray something good happens. For instance in Spain one time a nun asked me to pray for her mother who was dying of cancer. I went to the hospital to see her and discovered that she was very much afraid of dying. I had never met this woman before. So I went in to see her and told her I had come to pray. I told her that I believe that Jesus meant for us to pray for the sick. I told her that Jesus loved her and we were going to pray in his name. Her daughter, who had been with us in the hospital room, told me later that as soon as I walked out of the room her mother said to her "I never in my life felt the presence of Jesus the way I just did and you know what? I don't care if I die. I'm ready to die. I'm ready to die!' "A priest came to give her the Sacraments and he said later, "I never saw anyone look forward to dying like this woman." She wasn't healed of her cancer; she was healed of all her fear of dying.

On one of my many visits to Bilbao in northern Spain a priest asked me if I would go with him to see a young girl who was dying of cancer of the ovaries. So we went to the home of this girl named Lourdes who, I would guess, was about 14 years old. In Spain, when somebody is going to die, they are sent home from the hospital. If a person dies in the hospital, they are taken down to the chapel and there they have a little service and then it's off to the cemetery. So people try to bring their loved ones home to die. When we arrived she seemed near death and could barely speak above a very faint whisper. She was completely yellow from jaundice and had not been able to urinate for several days. She could not eat or drink anything without vomiting. Her mother, father and her brother were there and the priest who came with me. I said we were going to pray. They left me alone with her. I said they didn't have to but they left me alone with her for a few minutes. I told her about Jesus, how Jesus loved her, and that he healed people. And I told her we could pray and see if Jesus would heal her. I asked her if she would like to do that. She nodded yes. So I called her mother, father, brother, and the priest back into the room and asked them to gather around her and put their hands on her head. I had her mother put her hand on her stomach. Her brother was at the end of the bed and he put his hands on her feet. And so we prayed this way for 20 minutes or more. I then said, "I really have to go now; I need to get back to the group I'm with. I'm supposed to give a talk this afternoon." So we left.

Her family told me later that as I was going down the stairs of her apartment building she began to urinate, and then she said she was hungry. They fed her and she did not vomit. The next day she got up and told them she felt better and two days later she was on her feet and back to school.

Everyone was surprised because the doctors thought she had died and everyone at the school also thought she had probably died by then. At the school she kept telling all the kids, "Jesus loves me, he loves you, and he loves us all. Jesus is so good. He is so powerful. He healed me." This was in February or March. She kept talking about Jesus the rest of the school year and then in June she suddenly got very sick again and said, "Now I'm going to die, but it's okay. I'm giving Jesus my life for the young people of the world."

I never saw her again but her parents sent me this picture of her, which I still have and carry with me in my wallet. I have a brother with multiple myeloma, which of course, is very bad and he was here about a year ago now. I was telling him about how I had gone to pray with somebody here in New Hampshire who was quite sick with cancer and I told him about this little girl. I took out the picture and I said, "Here just hold her picture and we'll ask her to pray; I'm sure she's in heaven." My brother said, "May I see that picture?" So I took the picture out and put it in his hand and he's looking at this girl's picture and all of a sudden he said, "Leo, there's heat coming out of this picture! I tell you I can feel heat coming out of this picture." I said, "Well let's say a prayer. So we prayed and from that day on he's never had any back pain. They tell me that with his myeloma, he should be having a lot of back pain, but he doesn't. He goes out and exercises, and works around the yard and yet has no back pain. Apparently, his blood tests still shows multiple myeloma, but he has no symptoms and the doctors are amazed. I don't know what happened and can't give an explanation except to say I do know how powerful prayer can be.

Once I was giving a retreat for a large group of nuns from all around Spain. I was sitting at the table with three of these nuns one night having supper discussing the healings we had been talking about earlier. One of the nuns across from me was eating with her left hand and I jokingly said, "I think you're the first left-handed nun I've ever known." And she said, "I'm not really left-handed, I hurt my arm 14 years ago and I've had three or four operations. I'm going to have to have another one pretty soon because I can't use this hand anymore." So we finished supper, then I said, "Why don't we pray for your arm?" And she said, "No, no, no, no." She started walking away and I said, "Wait a minute, come here. Let's pray for your arm." And she said, "No." I said, "Why?" And she said, "Because there are too many more important things in the world, so many other people with real bad sicknesses. I'm getting by with my left arm. We don't have to pray for my arm." I said, "Look, if the Lord wants to heal your arm, it's for his glory—not yours. So why don't we say a prayer?" She put out her arm and said, "Do what you want!" She put her right arm out and I called over the other nuns and I said, "Let's pray for her." I got a letter from her weeks later and she said, "I must tell you what happened. You remember praying for my arm? I didn't want you to but you insisted. The next day my arm was tingling all day long. And on Sunday it was perfectly healed. I could write with it. I could work with it. I could do anything with it. It didn't hurt me anymore. When I got back to Barcelona, I went to the doctor. They took another X-ray and he asked me, 'What happened? We were going to operate; but it's perfectly okay.'" She closed her letter, "I just wanted you to know that my arm is perfectly healthy."

Some time later I had gone out to a convent in Zamora, another large city in Spain. When I arrived a couple of the nuns came out to the parlor to talk to me and they started asking me about the retreat that we had had. I told them it went well and added that there were even some healings, including the nun from Barcelona who could not use her right arm. One of the nuns said, "That's almost the same thing I have. I hurt my right arm and I can't use it anymore. The hardest thing for me to do is wringing the water out of a washcloth. I just can't turn my wrist. I used to play guitar but I can't anymore." She had come in limping so I asked her about that, and she said she had sprained her ankle.

"Well, why don't we pray for your arm?" I said. She said, "Go right ahead," and she put her arm on the table where we were sitting. I asked another nun to put her hands on the other nun's arm as we prayed. I just touched her hand and all of a sudden I felt something like an electric shock from my hand right into her arm. She jumped and I said, "Sister, your arm's okay now." She said, "I know. I just felt something all through my arm." I said, "Yes, you're all healed. I'll tell you something else," I said, "Your ankle's okay too; your ankle doesn't hurt anymore." I said, "Get up and walk." She got up and, sure enough, her ankle wasn't sore anymore. As soon as this happened the other nun said, "I'm out of here! I'm getting out of here! I don't know what's going on but I'm out of here."

I remember once at a retreat somebody had asked me to pray for her sister who was deaf. The woman was not there; she was at home. I don't know how deaf she was, but she had lost a lot of her hearing. I said, "Sure, we can do that." So I said, "You sit here in her place and we'll pray with you for your sister."

So we did that and later she told me, "You know what happened? At that very hour my sister was ironing at home and all of a sudden she stopped and she said, 'What is that noise?' Her son was there and said, 'What noise, I didn't hear anything.' He said, 'All I can hear is the refrigerator motor.' She said, 'Oh, that's what it is.' From that moment on she could hear."

These are just a few of the healings I can remember. In a few cases, like for that nun, I felt electric shock, but that didn't happen all the time. Sometimes I knew exactly when someone was healed and sometimes I didn't.

LILY TANEDO

Another story regarding a healing begins way back in 1941, when I was 12 years old. I was sick in bed and my sister gave me a Catholic monthly magazine for children called *Manna* that she had brought home from school. There was always a story at the end of the magazine of some young virtuous person who had died. That particular month it was about a Filipino girl named Lily Tanedo who had died at age 18. I used to read these stories regularly but for some reason that month I was more impressed than ever with this girl. I did not forget the name and to this day, I still have the magazine, the February 1941 issue.[16] I have often met people from the Philippines who know of her and some who even knew her family. And I always like to tell Filipinos about her whenever I meet them.

One day not long ago here at the Shrine I went out to take a walk and I saw two young women who looked Filipino. I went over and said hello and asked if they were from the Philippines. They said they were and were sisters; one lived nearby and the other was visiting from Oregon. I offered to take them on a tour of the Shrine. As we went up the hill one of them had a camcorder and was taking pictures and not looking where she was walking. Suddenly she stepped into a gully and twisted her ankle badly. Her camcorder went flying and she screamed, "My leg, my leg." I went over trying to decide what to do. I said, "I guess you can't get up. We have a golf cart down below. I could bring the golf cart up here and maybe if you could get up on the golf cart, I could drive you down. Otherwise the only other thing we can do is call an ambulance and have them back in here somehow and pick you up." She didn't answer and just kept crying in pain.

All of a sudden I thought of my friend from the Philippines, Lily Tanedo. So I bent down and I put my hands over her leg and I prayed, in silence, "Lily Tanedo. This is your Filipino sister. I don't think I have ever asked you anything like this before, but could you help me pray for her so that her leg will be okay?" Within a moment the young woman jumped up and said, "I'm all better." She got up and walked around and seemed fine. It was pretty dramatic because just a moment before she had been writhing in pain, but now she seemed fine.

---

[16] "Lily Tanedo: A Saintly Child of Our times" by Sr. M. Renata in *Manna: The Young Folks' Own Magazine*, 58(2), February 1941.

So I said, "You know I have to tell you something. I said a prayer for you to a Filipino girl who is in heaven. She's been a friend of mine for many years and I asked her to help me. And look what happened? I'm going to make a copy of a magazine article I have so you can know about her."

THE GIRL AND THE CROSS

One February day at a prayer meeting in Valladolid about 200 people were there and I happened to notice a young blond woman come in, a new person whom I did not know. After a short while she got up and went out and I thought, "Well, either she didn't like this or she had something to do." Anyway, she was gone.

We were in a gymnasium at a school. When we were finished and came out into the schoolyard it was getting dark. I saw in the corner of the schoolyard a figure of somebody who seemed to be leaning up against the wall crying. So I went over and to my surprise it was this blond girl. I asked her if there was anything wrong and she said, "My friend tried to commit suicide and she is very bad. She is in the hospital and they don't know if they are going to be able to save her life. I heard there was a prayer group here so I thought I would come and pray for her. But everyone was so happy singing and praying, and I was so sad. I just couldn't take it and I walked out." I said, "Don't cry. You know the Lord heals people." So I called a few of the people who were still there and asked them to pray with this girl for her friend. After we prayed for a short while we said our goodnights and went home.

The following week the same girl came back to the prayer group. She was all smiles and said, "Guess what? My friend is okay. She lived and she's okay." "See?" I said, "I told you the Lord heals people. Now you know."

The months went by and July came and I went up to Burgos to give an eight day retreat to the Marist Brothers. One day one of the brothers told me somebody was at the door asking for me. I was surprised because I didn't think anyone knew me in Burgos. I went to the door and there was a nun with a young girl; the nun asked if we could talk alone. She took me aside and said, "This girl tried to commit suicide several months ago. They don't know how she lived, but she made it. She is a friend of mine and she tells me she was angry when she woke up because she didn't want to wake up—she wanted to die. Now she's seeing a psychiatrist and taking medication. She told me yesterday that she's going to kill herself and this time nobody is going to save her." She continued, "I heard that you were here and I wondered if you could pray for her or with her." I didn't realize at the time that it was the very same girl that we had prayed for some 60 or 70 miles away in Valladolid back in February. She was studying at the University in Valladolid at the time. I said, "Well, Sister, it sounds like a rather difficult case, but I'll tell you what, I'll try if you will do me a favor." She said, "What?" I said, "You go in the chapel and pray." I brought her to the chapel and I said, "There's the Blessed Sacrament. You go pray over there and I'll talk to her."

The girl and I went to the parlor. She sat down on the couch and I said, "What's your name?" She told me her name, but would not look at me. So I said, "I'm from the United States and I have a cousin there with the same name you have, but she's a little older than you are." I was just trying to start a conversation but she wouldn't look at me. After several attempts at small talk, I said, "Sister seems to be worried about you. Do you know why?" She said, "Yes, I'm going to kill myself." "Oh," I said, "Why would you do that?" "Because it's not worth living," she said. I simply said, "Oh," not knowing what else I could say. I tried saying a few other things, but we were getting nowhere and she never looked at me so finally I said, "You know I'd like very much to help you but you're making it very difficult." Now she turned and looked at me and said, "I didn't ask you for anything. Leave me alone." I said, "I know, but now I know you so I love you and I would really like to help you because I love you. I really want to help you." Then I said, "Would you let me pray with you?" "Ha," she said scornfully, "I don't believe in that stuff. I don't have any faith." I don't know where the words came from, but I said, "That's okay; I have faith for the two of us." After I said that I worried that perhaps I should not have. In any case she shrugged and said, "Well, do what you want." I said, "I would like Sister to be here when we pray if you don't mind." She said, "No, I don't care."

I went into the chapel and called Sister out and asked her to come with me to pray. I asked her to put her hand on the girl's shoulder. I put my hands on the girl's head. She was sitting on a couch, and I began to pray. And after a few minutes she suddenly keeled right over and fell down onto the couch. So I put her legs up on the couch. The nun was frightened, thinking she had fainted. I asked the sister to remain calm and sit down. I took out my Rosary and made a sign to the nun to do the same and we just sat there saying the Rosary.

After ten or fifteen minutes or so, the girl suddenly sat up with a big smile on her face. Then she stood up, and with tears beginning to stream down her cheeks she came over to me and threw her arms around me, hugged me, and kept saying, "Thank you, thank you, thank you, thank you." I said, "Oh, don't thank me." I knew something had happened but I didn't know what. I said, "Don't thank me, thank God. He loves you." I then said, "I'm going to have to go to give a talk to the brothers. I'll walk you out to the car." As we walked out I noticed Sister's wooden crucifix that she was wearing, a small one, and I asked her where she got it because I was looking for one like that and I couldn't find one.

The following day the nun called me and said, "Wait till I tell you what happened. When we got in the car to leave yesterday, the girl said, 'Sister, I have to pray.'" They went back to the convent and into the Chapel and stayed there for four hours. The girl told the nun that when I put my hands on her head, she felt herself falling. The girl said, "I felt him putting my legs up on the couch and I could hear you going to sit down; I wanted to open my eyes, but I couldn't. I tried to move a finger but I couldn't, and then I heard a voice calling my name and saying, 'I'm stronger than you are. I am the way, the truth and the life.' She said, 'You see? I thought if I wanted to kill myself, nobody could stop me, not even God.' And then she said, 'I can't open my eyes, can't move a finger, and I'm so sure I heard that voice say, 'I'm stronger than you are. I am the way, the truth and the life.'"[17] So the nun said, "We prayed and then I said to the girl, 'Don't you think you should go home? Your parents will be worried about you.' So I took her home and I walked into the house with her. She walked in and right off said, 'Hi, Dad. Hi, Mom,' where before she wouldn't talk to anybody because she was so depressed. Right away they noticed something had happened, and they said to me, 'What happened?' I said, 'Let her tell you.' The girl asked, 'Is supper ready?' Her mother said, 'It's on the table. We've been waiting for you.' She went to sit down and her father said, 'Don't forget your medications.' She replied, 'Daddy, I don't need medications anymore.'"

After that retreat in July, I went back to the States. When I returned to Spain in September I had a little package and an envelope in the mail that contained a crucifix like the one the nun had. The package contained a letter from this girl that said, "I remember you telling Sister that you wanted a crucifix like hers so I found one for you. I am sending it to you so you won't forget me. I don't know why I'm living. I only know I have to live." I still have that cross and I wear it a lot of times, especially when I give my talks.

I began to ask around and I found out this young girl was studying law in the city where I was, though she came from Burgos. One day I met some students from the university and I asked if they knew her. By this time I knew her name and her family name because she had written to me. They said, "We know who she is, yeah!" I asked if they knew where I could find her. They told me the street where she lived with

---

[17] John 14:6.

some other girls, but they did not know the exact address. That was not very much to go on in a big city with half a million people.

A few weeks later I was walking to the center of the city and before I knew it, I found myself walking down the street where this girl lived. There were many big apartment buildings and I had no idea where she lived. There was one person I knew on the street so I went over to that house and inquired about any girls from the university who lived around there. At first she said no, but a moment later said "Wait a minute. See that doorway over there in that apartment building? I've seen girls go in there. Maybe that's where it is."

I went over to the doorway. It had many mailboxes and, to my amazement, one of them had her name on it and it said which apartment was hers. I ran upstairs, found the apartment and rang the bell. I could hear the bell ringing but nobody answered. Since it was 11:00 in the morning I thought she must be in class. I rang again, but again nobody answered. Content that I at least now knew where she lived, I turned around and started walking down the stairs and all of a sudden I heard the door open. I ran back up the stairs and there she was in the doorway standing there in her pajamas.

Of course, we had only seen each other once, several months before, so we greeted each other with a simple "Hi." She said, "I'm sick. I'm running a high fever. I was in bed and I wasn't going to answer the door, but you rang again so I thought I would come." I said, "Okay, go back to bed. Now I know where you live, I'll see you some other time." She said, "No, please come in. Would you mind?" We walked into the kitchen and sat down at the table across from each other. She looked at me and began to cry and said, "How come you came today?" She said, "This is the worst day I've had since the day that I saw you. I am so depressed and I'm feeling so sick." I said, with tears in my own eyes, "You know why I'm here? God loves you. Can't you see how much God loves you? I had not intended to come here today. I was going somewhere else. I don't even know how I got here. You tell me it's the worst day you've had since you saw me and all of a sudden I walk in? Do you think that's a coincidence? Can't you see how much God loves you?" She said, "Yeah, I guess so. I guess you're right!" So I said, "Go back to bed and I'll see you again some other time."

I did see her once after that. She came to my house one evening and we talked for a while and then I didn't see her again. After I left Spain I heard she had finished her studies and gone up to work in San Sebastian, way up north.

One day I had gone back to Spain with some American friends for the ordination of one of our boys and they wanted to take a trip up to Lourdes. We were going by the city where she lived so I found her apartment, but she wasn't there. A few years later somebody gave me some money to go back to Greece to give a retreat to the nuns I knew there. Before I left for the trip, I wrote to a friend and asked, "Would you see if you can find out something about this girl? Her parents used to live at this address in Burgos and she used to live at this address in San Sebastian." My friend got a friend in Burgos to go to the house, but her parents had moved and they were not there anymore. She got another friend in San Sebastian to go to the house where the girl was living and there was an elderly lady there who was the girl's mother and she said, "She has her own place now. I can give you the phone number."

When I got to Spain I called her and I told her who I was and asked her if she remembered. She said, "Yes." I said, "I would like very much to see you." So we arranged a meeting halfway between where she was and where I was because it was quite a long trip and she didn't want me to drive all the way. We went into a restaurant and had lunch together. I asked her what she was doing and she said, "I'm a lawyer. I have my own office and I have three lawyers working for me. I also give classes at the university." Then I said, "Do you remember what happened when we first met?" She's a shrewd lawyer, so she said, "Why don't you tell me? Tell me what *you* remember." So I went over the whole story about how we met, how at first she didn't want to talk to me. I told her about her friend coming to pray for her at the prayer meeting; she didn't know about that. She said, "What did she look like?" I told her and she said, "Oh, that was my best friend." I said, "Yes, we prayed for you and then later I met you and you were very depressed and didn't want to talk to me. When I prayed with you, you fell down and you heard a voice." I said, "Do you remember that?" She said, "Yes, I do. I still remember that voice. I can't tell you if it came from inside of me or outside of me, but I heard it. I know I did."

We talked more and she remembered all that had happened, and told me what she was doing. And I told her what I was doing and that I was back in the States. When we finished lunch at the very nice restaurant, I reached for my wallet and she said, "Oh no, no, no. Let me take care of this." Then we walked out to her car and I said, "You know, I have a very bad heart and I don't expect I'm going to live too much longer so I'll probably never see you again on Earth, but I will see you in heaven." And she said, "Oh, I don't know. I'm still not into religion." I said, "Do you remember you said to me that you didn't have any faith and I said that I had faith for the two of us? Well, I'm going to have enough prayer for the two of us, and I'm going to get you into heaven." I pulled out the crucifix that she had given me. It was under my sweater, and I said, "See this? You gave me that. Every day when I put it on, I pray for you. I love you very much. You don't know how much I love you and how much you mean to me, because you came into my life in such a very special way. God worked in you in such a special way when I prayed with you. You mean a lot and I love you, I'll never forget you and I'll always pray for you and I'll get you into heaven." She threw her arms around me and hugged me real tight for a long time and then she just let me go, ran to her car, started it up and sped away.

I had asked her for her address and she gave it to me and I wrote to her and sent a picture of me and said, "I would love to have a picture of you." She never answered. I wrote back and sent another picture and said, "I guess you didn't get the first one. I'd love to hear from you and get a picture." But she never answered. I had a friend in Spain who called her and had the hardest time and finally after many tries, many days, he finally got through. He said he got the impression that, while she was glad I thought about her, that that was about it. She didn't say she wanted to hear from me anymore. I think for some reason, I don't know what it is, she doesn't seem to want to keep in touch.

MARIO THE MECHANIC

I want to insist that the story about the girl and the cross, and all the other stories I am relating here are just to show how much God was working in my life through the power of the Spirit after I had opened my heart that day in Burlington on July 16, 1974. From that day on, as I'm trying to explain, the Lord was doing much more in my life and through my ministry than I had ever experienced before.

I remember in Spain we had a neighbor, an Italian named Mario, who was married to a Spanish woman, and who had an auto repair shop. He used to fix our cars and he was always good-natured, smiling and laughing. One day he got quite sick. Little by little he finally had to give up his repair shop. I used to speak to him every now and then, but if I tried to bring up religion, he would jokingly put me off, "Oh, I don't need that now." I couldn't talk with him seriously about religion, but I would go visit him after he became sick. He was a very good man. He used to be so happy to help me with my car and sometimes wouldn't ask me for any money. He was always helping everybody, but he just wasn't into going to church very much and he didn't want to talk about it.

One night I was on my way home and all of a sudden, I felt the Lord urging me to go see Mario and have him go to confession. So, I went over and I walked into the house and said to his wife that I wanted to see Mario. He was in bed. I asked his wife to leave us alone and close the door. When I called his name he immediately began to joke and laugh. I said, "Mario, no more, no more joking, no more laughing. This is serious. You are going to go to confession. All right? You're going to go to confession." "Oh no," he said, "All these years." I said, "I don't care, Mario! How many years?" I sat down and persisted saying, "More or less, how long has it been since you last confessed?" I don't remember what he told me but I said, "Okay now, let's go over things that maybe you might want to confess." So I asked him questions and asked him to tell me what he wanted to tell me and little by little he did and everything came out. At the end I said, "Okay, all you need is to be really sorry for all your sins. Are you?" He said, "Yes, yes." And I talked to him about God and God's love for him and how God wants him in heaven with him and he wants to forgive all his sins. I said, "As long as you're sorry he will forgive you." He said, "Okay, okay."

I gave him absolution and we said some prayers together and I said, "Now, Mario, I'm going home and I'll be right back. I'm going to bring you Communion." "Oh," he said, "It's been a long time." I said, "You just went to confession, so now you can go to Communion. I'll be back in ten minutes." So I went home. It wasn't too far away, and came back with Communion. I gave him Communion and we prayed. I don't remember whether I anointed him or not with the Sacrament of the Sick. I might have, but I'm not sure. In any case we said some prayers. By now his wife was overjoyed by all that was happening. So I said, "Goodnight, Mario, I'm going home now." It probably was 8:00 or 9:00 o'clock when I left him. I went home and later went to bed.

In the middle of the night—probably 1:00 in the morning—someone began banging on my door. I went to the door and it was some neighbors of his and they said, "Please come, Mario just died." So I went right over. His wife was in tears but at the same time so happy that I had gone over that night and had given him all the Sacraments. He was such a good man, but he just wasn't into religion. Why was it that *that* night I was so sure I had to go over and I had to get him to go to confession? I knew that I had to go. I didn't know he was going to die; I just knew I had to get him to go to confession and to receive Communion.

EXPRESSING THE INEXPRESSIBLE

I mentioned earlier that the first night after I had been prayed with, while in the chapel, I had begun to pray in tongues. I was very surprised and was not even sure what was happening to me when it began. It was kind of bubbling up in me and I knew it was the Spirit helping me to say what I couldn't say with ordinary words. I was trying to express my love and praise for God and was running out of words and all of a sudden they bubbled up in me, just gushed out of me. I really felt it was the Spirit of God in me, helping me to praise God with sounds. As St. Paul says in Chapter 8 of his letter to the Romans where he is talking about the Spirit of God living in us: "... the Spirit too comes to the aid of our weakness; for we do not know how to pray as we ought, but the Spirit itself intercedes with inexpressible groanings."[18]

After that first time I found that praying in tongues was not very difficult. Indeed, there is nothing miraculous at all about speaking in tongues. Praying in tongues is not conceptual prayer. In other words, we often express ourselves with a smile, humming, singing, moving our hands, jumping, and all sorts of nonverbal ways. People know we are happy or sad by our tears or our laughter. But we don't stop to think, "Oh, I think I'll laugh now," or "Right now I'll smile"—we just do it without thinking. It's non-conceptual. In the same way, why wouldn't we be able to pray and express ourselves to God, not only conceptually, but in other ways too? You don't have to think about everything you're going to say to God. Why can't it be spontaneous and sometimes with sounds that are not words? In the same way you might walk down the

---

[18] Romans 8:26.

street humming and people would say, "Well, look at how happy he is." I really believe that this is one way of looking at this gift of tongues. It is such a help when you don't know what else to say to God.

Allowing yourself to speak in tongues is also a help when you're praying for something. There are times when you are praying for something and you don't really know what you're praying for, exactly what you need, and so turn to tongues and say, "Lord, I'm not sure what's going on here but I'm going to pray in tongues and you take over." There were many such experiences in my life, but one I remember very well.

I had come home from Spain and was visiting one of my brothers, and his son and wife, and their children had come over. We had a nice afternoon with a picnic at the house on the lake. They had heard I had gotten involved with Charismatic prayer and that I even prayed for healings. My niece through marriage, whom I had just met that day, said, "Will you pray for our little boy?" He had some kind of medical problem. I said, "Yes, we could do that."

The little boy was so small I did not want to frighten him by saying, "We're going to pray for you," because children wonder what this is all about and could easily become frightened. Instead I went off with this young family apart from the others. I explained to my nephew and his wife and their three young children that we were going to pray together and we were going to pray for each other. For the children I made it a sort of game. I said, "All right? Whom will we pray for first?" One of the children said, "Daddy." So we said a prayer for Daddy. We prayed this way, going from one member of the family to another until we came to the child who had the problem.

As we were praying for him, I suddenly got what I might call a revelation. We finished the prayer and I said, "Okay, you all go back, but I want to talk with Mommy alone." When the others left I said, "What is there in your life about swings?" And she was very surprised. "Oh my goodness," she said. "I don't know how you know that, but I can't get on a swing. I'm so afraid to get on a swing. I always have been afraid of swings. But why would you know that?" I said, "Well, the Lord told me, I guess."

"But why?"

I said, "I don't know. All I do know is that in Christ there is nothing to be afraid of, so we're going to pray about that." So I sat there and probably held her hand or put my hand on her shoulder and began to pray. I was praying very quietly, but I could tell that nothing was happening. At first I didn't know what to do, but then it came to me: "I'll let the Holy Spirit take over and I'll pray in tongues." But I did not want to frighten her because I didn't know if she knew anything about this, so I began to pray in tongues but very, very softly. I wasn't even sure she could hear me. I had my eyes closed and when I finished, I opened my eyes, glanced at her and she was in tears and she said, "Oh, that was so beautiful, that was so beautiful."

Well, then I knew something had happened so I said, "Well, just thank God for whatever it is he is doing or wants to do. Just say, 'Thank you.'" She said, "We have to get going. We have to get home." They lived several miles away. So they left and I stayed there with my brother and sister-in-law. The next morning, I was still in bed because I slept in a little late. I heard the phone ring and a minute later I heard my sister-in-law at my door saying, "Are you awake? It's my daughter-in-law on the phone and she wants to talk to you."

I picked up the phone next to my bed and it was this mother I had prayed with the day before and she said, "Uncle Leo, I want to thank you for yesterday. It was so beautiful. It just changed my life. I was telling my husband about it and what happened and he's so amazed too." Then she said, "You do know what happened, don't you?" I said, "Well, I know we prayed and I guess you felt better." "Well, it wasn't just that," she said, "You began to pray in tongues, didn't you? Is that what you were doing?" I said, "Well, yes." She said, "You don't know this, I guess, but I have a grandmother who was Indian,

Native American, so that kind of thing interests me." She said, "I heard you speaking in Indian and I know what you were saying. You were saying something like this, 'I love you and I want you to trust me and I will take care of everything. Believe in me, trust me and believe that I love you and I will take care of everything else.'" That was more or less the basic message.

Then she said, "You see, about the swings. Not only was I afraid of swings all the time, but in my life I often felt like I was on a swing and one moment I was swinging right up to God and the next moment I was swinging far away from God. But that's all gone now. That's gone and I'm just with God." She said, "So, I just wanted to thank you because it's so beautiful and it has just changed my life and I'll never forget this." She still reminds me of that and that had to be well over 20 years ago. So there again is another sign of something the Lord is doing through the power of his Spirit. These gifts of the Holy Spirit that I just hadn't even realized were mine, if I wanted them. These gifts of the Spirit are readily available to any Christian. They are for all of us, for the good of one another, and we should be willing to accept them and use them.

HEALING LOVE

Let me tell you about one of the most beautiful healings that I have ever seen. I had come home from Spain for the summer and I was helping in a parish in my hometown. One day a young woman came into the sacristy and said to me, "Oh, Father Leo, would you pray for me?" She was crippled. She'd had polio when she was young girl and her right leg was twisted and her right hip was a lot higher than the other one. She said that she could move her knee cap around, and when she walked she was almost walking on the outside edge of her foot. She also limped badly and had pain in her leg, especially the top of her leg, if she stood for very long. She was a schoolteacher and she said she could only be on her feet a short time and then she had to sit down because her leg hurt. She had a couple of children and said how the first birth had been very, very difficult because of the way her body was. The second time she was pregnant we had prayed for her in the prayer group and it was a very easy birth.

During this conversation in the sacristy she said, "Do you know what happened to me the other day? My little boy knows that I can't run and he thinks that it's funny that he can run and I cannot. So he ran off away from me right out onto the highway. I was so afraid that he was going to get hit by a car. So I hope you'll pray for us."

I was so struck with how sad this woman's life was because of her deformity. I said, "Did you ever ask God to heal you?" She said, "Heal me? You don't think God's going to heal me, do you?" And I said, "Why not? God can do anything." "I know" she said, "But, you see the way I am, crippled like this, and I've been like this for twenty years." I said, "Look, God can do anything and he told us to pray, so what have we got to lose?" She said, "If you want to pray, go right ahead. I'll let you pray." I said, "Well, I think this might take some time because, as you say, it seems like a rather difficult case so it may take a little more time than usual. When could I see you?" She said, "Well, why don't you come over to my house for supper some night?" She said, "Bring your mother and come over." I agreed and we made a date.

My mother and I went over and her mother was there with her husband and children. We had a nice meal and after we finished eating I suggested we go into the parlor and pray. I had her lie down on the couch and I got everybody to gather around her and we laid hands on her and began to pray. We prayed for quite a while and at one point I asked her, "Have you noticed anything at all?" Sometimes people notice something happening. She said she didn't feel anything so we prayed a little more.

After praying for a while longer I said, "I think that's enough for this time, but before I go back to Spain, if you'd like, maybe we could get back together again and pray some more." I went home and the next day she called me. She said, "You know, last night when you asked me if anything had happened and I said, 'No,' well I didn't want to tell you because I couldn't believe it myself, but I had felt a tug in my hip. After you had gone I checked and, sure enough, my hips are even now. So much so that I am going to have to change all my slacks because I had one leg longer than the other. Now they're about the same length so I'm going to have to change them." "Well, good," I said, "That's a good sign, and I think that means we should keep on praying." She said, "Okay, how about coming over for supper again." So we made another date for a week or two later and again I went with my mother.

After we had eaten I again had her lie down on the couch and we began to pray. We prayed for a while and I didn't feel that anything was happening so I said, "May I ask you some questions? Is there anybody that you have not forgiven?[19] God says, 'I want to love you but I want you to love other people too.' Now if you're going to close the door and say, 'No, I'm not going to love them or forgive them,' you're kind of closing the door to what God would like to do. I want to be sure that there is nobody whom you don't love or that you have not forgiven." She said, "No, I can't think of anybody." I said, "Well, okay, just close your eyes and let's pray."

We began to pray and ask the Lord to help us out, to tell us if there was anything that he wanted us to do or that he wanted us to know, and all of a sudden she opened her eyes and said, "Now I do remember something, but I don't know if it's very important. When I was eight years old, and I was crippled with polio and had to walk with crutches and my parents sent me away in the summertime to camp for handicapped children, and I remember when we went down to the square in town and they put me on the bus, and I noticed

---

[19] I have found in this ministry that it is always a lot easier to be healed if you have forgiven other people, but if you don't forgive someone it's like closing a door.

all the other kids were in wheelchairs; and I said, 'I don't want to go.' I can walk with crutches. They're in wheelchairs, why should I go with them? My mother said to me, 'Yes, yes, you go. It'll be good for you. You're going to like it.'" She said, "I got the impression my mother just wanted to get rid of me. That she was finding it hard to see me this way, so crippled, and to take care of me and so maybe she wanted to get rid of me for a couple of weeks. That's what I felt. Like I was being sent away." Then she added, "That really hurt, but I had forgotten all about that."

I said, "Well, maybe the Lord is bringing it back now for a reason. Close your eyes again and be eight years old and try to imagine yourself back there and getting on the bus and try to see Jesus there with you." So I prayed with her asking Jesus to be with her and help her understand that, yes, maybe it was difficult for her mother and father. Maybe it was a bit of a relief to have her away for a little while. After all, they are human beings and she might need help to understand that and if there was anything to forgive, to be able to forgive them. So we did that and I said, "Do you feel you really forgive them?" She said, "Yes, I do." Then we prayed a little more.

After that night her leg straightened out a little bit more and she said that her kneecap didn't move around anymore. She was very excited and said how much easier it was to climb stairs and how much better she looked and felt. I said, "Maybe before I go back to Spain we could get together one more time." So I visited her and her family one more time with my mother and again I had her get on the couch and we began to pray. We prayed for a while and I said, "This is not working. Something is wrong. Something is in the way. I'm not sure what it is. Just keep quiet everybody and ask the Holy Spirit to help us out."

So we kept quiet and I tried to listen to what the Lord might want to say and all of a sudden—this will make you laugh—I said, "Oh, I know what it is." She opened her eyes and said, "What?"

I said, "You have to love your leg."

"What?"

"You have to love your leg, that bad leg you have. You have to love it."

"Oh no, I can't do that!"

I said, "Now listen, God loves you the way you are and he's asking you to love yourself the way you are." She said, "I'm sorry, I cannot. Do you realize it's been at least twenty years or more that I have been crippled like this? And now you want me to say it's okay? I love myself this way?"

I got up and said, "Well, then, we're all done. There's nothing more to be done." She said, "No, no, please. This has been going so well I wish we could keep going." I said, "But you have shut the door. God, through his love, wants to come with his love to you and you're saying 'No. You can't love me this way. I can't love myself this way,' so you just shut the door."

She looked at me with tears in her eyes and said, "You don't know what you're asking me." She was crying and she said, "The other day my little boy said to me, 'Mommy, you're not like other ladies. You have ugly legs.' My little boy said that to me. Now you're asking me to say it's okay, I love myself this way?" I said, "Yes, I am."

"I can't," she said. Then I felt badly for her and I said, "All right, you can't. Jesus once said that without him you can't do anything, but with him you can." I knelt down and said, "Okay, Lord, unless you help her to do this, she can't do it. You said we couldn't do anything without you so now come and help her to do what she cannot do by herself." So we just sat there and prayed a little bit and all of a sudden she looked down at her leg, tears streaming down her face and she said, "Leg, I love you." As she said that, the foot that she used to walk on the side of straightened out.

I love to tell that story because we can learn so much from it. Not only that God can heal and wants to heal, that's one thing you learn, but that we have to help and cooperate with God. And one way is to forgive others as much as we can. We may find it difficult so ask for help from him to forgive others. And forgiving doesn't mean, "Oh I feel great." No, it can be very difficult. But if we can at least say, "I really *want* to forgive," I think God will honor that. Forgiving others is critically important, but so is forgiving and loving yourself. So many people hate themselves or think they're such great sinners, and say to themselves, "I'm no good," and "God can't love me the way I am." You see, when we take that attitude *we* close the door, not God. God can love anybody just as they are, so just let him love you and believe and forgive yourself. I think maybe everybody has to learn to forgive themselves because we've all made mistakes, all of us. We're all sinners. And, although God is quite willing to forgive anything and everything, sometimes we're not. When we think we're too sinful to be forgiven by God that's a form of pride. It is pride to think that I'm so bad even God can't forgive me. You're giving yourself a lot of importance if you think you're that bad. You're not that bad. God can forgive anybody. So don't be so proud. Just be humble and say, "I goofed up; I fouled up. If God can forgive me and love me anyway, I'll do the same for myself." And that really can change so many lives. I'm convinced of that and I've seen that when I've spoken with many people.

TRANSFORMATION

I used to be invited to give talks to nuns in Spain, especially cloistered nuns. There are a lot of cloistered convents and they were rather neglected because most didn't have their own chaplains. They would try to get priests to come and say Mass, usually some old retired priest, but they really didn't have a priest that they could consult for spiritual direction. When they found out I was available, I was invited to come.

One time I went to a Carmelite convent in a little village where I had been once before. When I got there in the morning they said to me, "We hope you don't mind, but we have invited a friend—this woman from another village who comes here now and then and runs errands for us because, of course, being cloistered, we don't leave the convent. So we always look for some good woman to run errands for us. She has quite a story and we thought she'd enjoy listening to you." I said I didn't mind at all.

After I gave my talk it was time for lunch. The nuns passed out food for us through a turntable there and the woman and I had a little parlor together where we ate our lunch. While we were eating she said to me, "I enjoyed your talk very much. I think maybe you'd understand what I'd like to say to you." She continued, "When I was just a little girl the civil war was going on here in Spain. There was the 'right' and the 'left' and the right consisted of the rich and unfortunately, the Church, and all the powerful. The left was mostly the poor and students. They hated each other and so they each had their own army. One army would come into a village and look for their enemies and just shoot them. They'd leave and the other army would come in and shoot the others." One day the army on the right came into her village and they said to the priest, "Are there any communists here?" The priest told them that this girl's father had said something against the Church or the government. As a result, they took him out and shot him.

She told me she was only about three years old when this happened. She said that her mother had always been a very good Catholic, but her mother just could not go back to church. How could anybody go to church and listen to a priest preaching when you knew he had your husband shot? This girl had older brothers and sisters and they knew what had happened and they were very critical of the Church and of religion.

As a little girl she heard all this, so she too began to think and speak critically of the Church the way the others did. When she got to be around seven years old her mother said, "Now it's time for you to make your First Communion. They're going to give classes at the church. So you go." And the girl said, "I don't want to go." But her mother insisted, so she had to go. She said, "I went but I would listen to all this and later I would say to the other kids, 'Don't believe it. It's all lies.' And the teachers would get angry with me and say, 'You're bad.' And I was glad when they said I was bad, really glad." "But," she said, "Sometimes I would go into the church and I would go up near the tabernacle and I would say, 'Jesus, are you there? Are you really there?' "In Spanish, she would say, "*Di, di,*" which means "Tell me!" Of course, she never heard an answer so she said, "See, it's all lies."

She made her First Communion because she was forced to and then when it was time to make her Confirmation her mother insisted that she do that too. Finally, when she was twelve or thirteen years old she decided, "That's the end of religion for me." A few years went by and one day another girl told her a certain young man was in love with her. She said, "I watched him and I realized that he went to church regularly. I was curious so one day he asked me to go with him for a walk or something, so I went just out of curiosity. What kind of guy is this who goes to church? He was so nice, really a nice guy. We fell in love and planned to get married. I didn't tell him what I thought about religion but we got married in the church. I guess that was the only way. After we were married he would say on Sunday, 'What Mass are we going to go to?' And I would always find an excuse and I would say, 'Why don't you go to this Mass and I'll go to another one later because I want to work on my dinner today and I'll go later' or else, 'I already went, so you go now.'" She added, "He had a lot of devotion to the Virgin Mary and at night he would say, 'Would you like to say the Rosary with me?' And I'd say, 'Rosary? That's so boring. No, not that.'"

It didn't take too long for him to realize how she really felt about the church. She told him frankly, "Look, I don't believe any of that stuff. After all, a priest had my father shot and that's the end of that."

She went on, "We had three children. And one day my mother died. When I saw my mother's body in the coffin, I thought, if there's no God, there's no heaven." Then she said,

"There's got to be a God, at least for my mother." So she said, "I've got to find out if there's a God. I started looking for God but I didn't know how to find him. There was a nun working in the village, so I went to see her and I said, 'I want to know God. Can you help me?' So she gave me a book by Brother Raphael, who had been a Trappist Monk in a monastery not far away and had died rather young and had written a lot of things before he died."

She didn't have a lot of education but she liked this brother's writings because they were simple and because she liked "his God." So she said to her husband, "Bring me to the monastery where he's buried. I want to pray at his tomb." Her husband said, "Why? You don't go to church, you don't pray, and now you want to go over there?" She said, "Yes, bring me." So he drove her over and she said, "I knelt at Brother's tomb and I said, 'Brother Raphael, I want to know God. I like your God. I want to know your God. Could you help me? Could you pray for me?'" Nothing.

On her way back home she was thinking, "Now what do I do?" Then she remembered a friend who had been asking them to make a Cursillo.[20] When she got home she called him up and said, "Look, I want to make one of those Cursillos. I want to make it this weekend." He said, "No, no, no, you can't. There is one, but it's already all booked." She said, "I've done favors for you before. You've got to get me in there." He agreed to try and later that day he called her back and said, "Boy, are you lucky! Somebody cancelled out so you can go."

So on Friday her husband drove her to the retreat house run by the Jesuits where the Cursillo was to be held. Her husband left her there and then went home. She said she went to the talks and listened to everything they were saying but it didn't mean anything. All day Saturday, she listened to all the

---

[20] The word *cursillo* means "short course" in Spanish. The Cursillo movement started in Spain in 1944 and is designed to raise up and train leaders for the Church.

talks but, again, it didn't mean anything. Sunday morning she started with them again, and nothing happened.

Finally, after lunch, there was going to be one more talk before they left but she decided not to go. Instead, she went off to the chapel by herself. She said, "I knelt in the chapel and said, 'Lord, look. I came here this weekend because I wanted to know you. Where are you? If you really exist, if you really are, please let me know, because I want to know." Once again she felt no response so she said to herself, "It's no use." She got up and went to her room, packed her suitcase, and sat on the bed and waited for her husband to come and get her.

"Just then," she said, "the whole room filled with light—bright, bright light. And out of that light there were rays of light coming right to me and into my heart, my chest. These rays of light just went right into me. And, right there I knew God. All of a sudden I just *knew* God. And what I knew was that God loved me. He loved me so much and he loved the whole world. God is love and loves and loves and loves and all he wanted was to love me and to love everybody. I don't know how long I sat there like that but all of a sudden the light was all gone, but now I knew God. I jumped up and I ran down to the hall where the priest was talking to the people and I began to scream, 'I know God, I know God. He loves me. He loves so much and he loves you, and he loves you, and he loves everybody! He loves us all.'"

The priest tried to get her to be quiet since he was trying to give a talk. As much as she insisted she had to tell everyone what had just happened to her, he insisted that she sit down quietly. She said, "I sat down but it was so hard to be quiet." And years later people who were there said the only thing they remembered about the whole weekend was what she was saying.

Eventually her husband arrived to take her home. Later he told me, "We were driving home and she's talking to me about God. And I'm driving and I'm thinking, 'This is not my wife; my wife doesn't know these things. My wife cannot say these things. I've got the wrong woman.'" And he said, "I'd glance over at her and I'd say, 'It sure looks like her! But it can't be her.'" When they got home, for the next two or three weeks he couldn't go near her. She'd say, "Hey, I'm your wife." And he'd say, "Just stay away from me." He told me, "I couldn't go near her. I couldn't touch her because it was like touching God. I was scared."

Since they had a small business they were able to afford to have a girl come to the house every Monday to help clean and do various chores. The girl came in Monday as usual and then went home. On Tuesday the girl came back crying. She said, "Please tell me, what happened to you last weekend?" The woman said, "Why do you ask?" She said, "Because when I came to work yesterday and I looked at you, I saw God in your face. You have God in your face!" She explained further, "When I went home I was going to tell a lie to my mother, but I couldn't because I kept seeing your face." Then she said, "I went out with the other kids and I was going to say some bad words, but I couldn't. I can't do anything wrong because I keep seeing God in your face. Please tell me what happened."

This couple—this woman especially—got to be very good friends of mine and I want to insist that they are very normal people. They have a great sense of humor. She's a great cook. Good, normal children. This is a part of their story that they have told to very few people and is one reason why I am not using their names.

REASSURANCE

St. Maria Goretti was killed by a man named Alessandro Serenelli on July 6, 1902 in Ancona, Italy while resisting rape. She was canonized in 1961. On the hundredth anniversary of her death—July 6, 2002—I was getting ready to say Mass. I was thinking of St. Maria Goretti and of

I AM THE HOLY LAND … *and so are you*

the fact that I had to go into the hospital in a few days. The doctors were going to begin to try to repair the aneurysms I have because they were getting too big and were in danger of bursting. Naturally, I was nervous and anxious, and afraid of this whole procedure, thinking perhaps I might die. I was thinking, "I hope God has forgiven me all my sins. I hope I have been open enough and sincere enough in confessing my sins in my life. I hope that all my sins are forgiven. I know that he is a good God and forgives. I just hope that I let him know I was sorry for my sins and I hope that that's done."

It was a Saturday morning and usually when I say Mass on Saturday morning the only one there with me is Fr. Joe Ross, who concelebrates with me. But this day there were others there, including our superior and another priest. I was the celebrant and when it came time to put the wine and water in the chalice, Fr. Ross handed me the wine and I put some in the chalice and he handed me the water and I put a few drops in, said the offering and then I turned around, after the prayer to wash my hands. He was there and he poured the cruet with the water but no water came out. He again tipped it higher, almost straight up and still no water came out. Then he shook it up and down to try to get at least a drop out, but not even a drop came out. So I thought, "Well, there's no more water. If I don't wash my hands, the Mass is still valid, so I'll just go on with the Mass." So I went back and he put the cruets back on the table and I continued the prayers of the Mass, but at the same time I was thinking, "That's strange. I just took a few drops of water out of the cruet, and I know I took them out of the top of the cruet, just a few drops. I was so sure there was more water in there." Then I realized that the prayer we say as we wash our hands, "Lord, wash away my iniquities and cleanse me of my sins." I thought, "I wonder if God is telling me not to worry about my sins."

When we finished, Father Superior came over and said, "What was that all about with the cruets?" Fr. Ross said, "I went to wash his hands and there was no more water." He said, "What do you mean, there was no more water? I filled that cruet myself just before Mass. He took it in his hands and said, "Look!" And he poured water from the cruet right into the palm of his hand. There was water dripping off his hand and there was still more than half in the cruet. The other priest who was visiting said to me, "Well, Max, I guess God's trying to tell you that you don't have to worry about any sins." And Fr. Ross said, "You know, I was thinking that too." I didn't dare say, "So was I."

I have always felt that somehow St. Maria Goretti obtained that favor for me that day. I really believe that God was saying to me, "Stop worrying about your sins." This is just one more thing that I thank God for.

ANGELS?

I have some friends in Vermont who are very, very good Christians. They prayed a lot together as a family. Two of their children had cancer, but both recovered, one of them miraculously. The doctors had given up hope for her and yet, through prayer, she was healed. Even the doctors were surprised and wouldn't believe that she was healed, making comments like "She may feel better now, but she'll be back." Yet years later she is still free of cancer.

This family was very grateful to God and wanted to help others so they added a couple of rooms on to their house, which was on the outskirts of their town. They built a ramp so that they could bring wheelchairs into those extra rooms. The mother and wife, being a nurse, wanted to care for dying people, especially people dying of cancer. They would not take any money.

One day somebody gave them a rather large statue. I'm not sure if the statue was of Mary or St. Francis. So they thought, "We'll put that in the back yard, where the people sitting in the window could look out and see the statue all day." They thought, "We should really put a rock under it so that the grass won't grow around it." One day the woman was driving down the road near Middlebury with a friend. As they drove they suddenly saw a rock on the side of the road. This woman said, "I just saw a rock that looks like what we're looking for to put in the back yard underneath the statue." So she stopped and backed up on the side of the road and the two women got out of the car, opened the trunk and tried to lift the rock to put it in the trunk, but they could not lift it. Then they said, "Now what do we do?" Just then a young man showed up on a bicycle. He might have been 14 or 15. They hadn't seen him coming but all of sudden there he was and he very politely asked if he could help them. So he picked up the heavy rock as though it weighed nothing and put it very gently into the trunk of the car and said, "There you are." They said, "Thank you very much." He said, "Oh, that's okay, just do something for someone else when you can." They thought that was a little strange coming from such a young man.

When they returned home my friend said to her husband, "I have a rock in the trunk of the car that I think will do well under the statue in the backyard. Would you get the rock out?" He told me himself that he noticed that the back of the car was lower than it normally was due to the weight of the rock. And he could not lift the rock out of the trunk. Her husband—a big man over six feet tall—could not lift the rock out. So he called a few other men and between them, three or four of them, they were able to pick it up, drop it on the ground and roll it over and over into the back yard where it is now.

When he came into the house he said to his wife, "Who did you say put that rock in the car?" And she said, "Oh, this young boy that we met on the road." He said, "How could he? I could not lift it and it took three of us just to get it out and let it fall to the ground." So she said, "Well I guess it must have been an angel." And I think she's right—maybe it was. How else can you explain anything like this? I don't think this kind of thing happens to just anybody, because I think it needs to be people who understand God's ways and believe. To have faith and say, "I don't know who else it could have been but an angel."

RESTLESS SOULS

In the late 1950s when I was going to different schools around New England for vocation work, I once visited friends in Maine—a wonderful Christian couple with twelve children. They were very good people, very good Catholics; hardworking, very normal people in every way. Some of their children, by the time I stopped, were already grown up and some had already married and left. In order to have enough money for all their expenses, besides his job in some factory, they had added a greenhouse to the back of the house and they were selling flowers and plants.

The day I stopped we were sitting at the kitchen table talking and the wife said, "Oh, I have to tell you something that happened a few days ago. My sister down in Massachusetts committed suicide. We went to the funeral and came back and, a few days later in the middle of the night, I heard an awful noise, crashing, sounding like broken glass. What it sounded like was that somebody was breaking up our greenhouse.

"Of course, I woke up and I woke my husband and he ran downstairs, put all the lights on and looked all around and the noise had stopped, and everything was fine and nothing was broken. He came back and said, 'Maybe you were dreaming but, everything's fine.'" The next night the husband was working at the factory and she was alone and she heard the noise again. This time she went down herself, looked around and again everything was all right.

The third night it happened again and her husband was there. He went down again, came back and, once again, said everything was all right. Then she said, "Well, I know what it is. My sister needs some prayers."

When they got up the next day she went down to the parish, had some Masses said for the repose of her sister's soul, and they never heard any noise again.

I think this kind of thing only happens to people who know how to interpret it. These people were not only good Catholics with a lot of faith, but had a lot of understanding of the power of prayer. If this kind of thing happens, it's because God is trying to say something and you need to interpret it correctly. You see, the way to die is like an apple on a tree, when it's ripe, it falls off and when we get old enough and we're ready, we just go from this life to another life. But when you die violently, even accidentally, in some violent way it is possible that the soul is not resting in peace. Being members of the mystical body of Christ we all can contribute to each other. Jesus says in the Gospel of St. John, "I am the vine, you are the branches." He doesn't say, "I am the trunk, you are the branches." He is the vine. He is the whole thing. And we are branches in him and through him so that we contribute to each other. In the mystical body you have people in heaven. You have people maybe who have died but are not in heaven yet, even though it's hard to speak that way because there is no time once you die, but somehow you are not with God yet. And then there are people on Earth who are still praying, suffering, gaining merits—you could say it that way—and can contribute to one another and to people who may have died and still need help. And the ones who are in heaven who may pray for us. We are all branches on that same vine that is Jesus Christ.

SERAPIO THE SHEPHERD

I remember a priest in Spain who—if I may put it this way—got hit by the Holy Spirit and met Jesus Christ in the new way I have been describing. He said, "I open the Bible and it is as though somebody changed this book around. This is a new book."

Here's another story to illustrate what I mean. Right across the street from our place in Spain there lived a rather elderly man who had been a shepherd in his younger years, taking care of the sheep out in the field for many years. His name was Serapio and he had very little education. I don't know if he even knew how to read or write—probably not. He loved to talk about his life and his experiences and one day sitting down with him I said, "Can you tell me some things about sheep?"

"Of course. What do you want to know?"

"In the Bible there are things about sheep like where Jesus says, 'I am the Good Shepherd. I know my sheep and my sheep know me.'[21] Is that true? Do sheep really know their shepherd?"

"Oh, yes," he said. And he began to tell me how he knew every one of his sheep because when you spend all your time over many months with them you get to know that they are all different. "One likes to play more, one likes to fight more, one likes to run away. They are different," he said. "You get to know them and sometimes you give them names, and, of course," he said, "they get to know you."

Then I asked, what about where Jesus says, "I am the good shepherd; the good shepherd lays down his life for the sheep?"[22]

"Well," he said, "I almost had to give my life once." He told about how a couple of wolves came and took one of his sheep and he had to go after them to rescue the sheep. Up to this point it seemed that he was corroborating everything Jesus said about shepherds and sheep.

Then I got to where Jesus said, "What man among you, if he has a hundred sheep and has lost one of them, does not leave the ninety-nine in the open pasture, and go after the one which is lost, until he finds it?"[23] And he looked at me

---

[21] John 10:14.
[22] John 10:11.
[23] Luke 15:4. Also Matthew 18:12.

with a funny expression and said, "Well, no, not that. No shepherd would do that." When I seemed surprised to hear this he was almost apologetic and said, "I'm sorry, but it's not that I want to go against the word of God but, you see, if you left 99 sheep alone, you'd lose them *all*." He said, "Sheep are very stupid animals and they can't be alone and still be safe, so you'd lose them all. If you left 99 to go after just one lost one that would be *locura*." The Spanish word *locura* comes from *loco*, which means "crazy." That would be folly, foolish, stupidity, however you want to translate it.

Later that day when I got home I was still thinking about what my shepherd friend had said. I began to look at different commentaries on the Bible until I found what I thought was the right explanation. One author was saying, "You see, God, because he loves us so much, does foolish things. Even St. Paul says, dying on the cross, "For the Greeks, that is folly and for the Jews, it's a shame, something shameful. For us it's the wisdom and Power of God."[24] In other words, because God loves us so much he does something that no one in his right mind would do. He comes to share our lives. He leaves heaven to share life on Earth. Imagine coming here to share this kind of life, which always entails suffering and dying. But you see, when you are very much in love, you do foolish things. So this is the folly of God: love so profound that he would do what no shepherd would ever do.

Another day I went back to see him and I said, "I notice when the shepherds leave the village in the morning they go ahead of the sheep, but when they come back at night, they come behind the flock. Why do they go in front in the morning and behind at night?"

He smiled and answered, "Oh, that's easy. In the morning you have to go in front so that you can see if there are any dangers ahead. You go ahead and make sure that it's okay for them to come that way, that they won't fall off a cliff or run out in the road and get hit by traffic, or go in the wrong

---

[24] This is a paraphrase of 1 Corinthians 1:18-31.

field and eat somebody's vegetables; so you go ahead and they follow you and they go where you go. But when you come back at night they know where they're going and you go in the back to make sure they all get home." And I thought, This is exactly what Jesus does for us! He went ahead of us even in death. In all our sufferings, in all our tears and all our agony, pains and trials. Jesus went ahead of us and we follow. But when it's time to come home, to come back, to come to heaven; he goes behind to make sure we all get there. Jesus makes sure there are no stragglers.

In the book of Isaiah there is this passage:

"Here is the Lord Yahweh coming with power,
his arm subduing all things to him,
the prize of his victory is with him,
his trophies all go before him."[25]

The Bible ends up in The Revelation to John with "all those in new Jerusalem," meaning all those who are saved, coming into heaven as beautiful as a bride. And Jesus comes behind and says to his Father something to the effect of, "Look, here are my trophies, my reward. I won them by my victory on the cross. I'm bringing them home where they belong." There, again, was something I came to understand that I had never seen before. And I realized what was in Isaiah, that the desert becomes like a garden, where it was all dry becomes water, and that I myself, despite my dryness, whatever evil or shortcoming, have become a holy land because the Holy Spirit is really that rain from heaven that brings new life to all of us.

---

[25] Isaiah 40:10. See also Isaiah 62:11. These passages using the word "trophies" are from the *Jerusalem Bible* translation which is the translation I used most. The Hebrew word *sakar* is most often translated as "recompense" or "reward," but I like this translation best. The emphasis in the text is mine.

PLEASING GOD

We know from the word of God and from our own experiences that God is love and God loves us very, very much. We also should understand that God is very easy to offend and that's because he loves so much. When you love very, very much you're easy to hurt. Now we don't exactly hurt God, but you know how easy it is to offend someone who loves very much. However, there is another side to that and I want to tell how I learned about it.

One day in Spain I visited a couple I had married. By this time they had a little boy who had just learned to walk and was learning to talk. The father was busy at his office and the mother was in the kitchen getting lunch ready so I said, "Why don't I take the little boy for a walk outside?" So I took the boy for a walk and, of course, being a little boy, he just wanted to touch everything and run everywhere. All of a sudden he saw a flower, maybe a dandelion, but it was fading and falling apart. He was able to say,

flor, which means flower. So he picked it with his scrubby, dirty little hands and he held it up to me and said, "See, *flor*." I said, "Yes." And I added, "We're going home now but when we get home and Mommy opens the door you say to her, 'For you, Mommy.'" I said, "Can you say that?" And I taught him how to say it. When we got to the house, I rang the bell and she opened the door with her apron on from getting lunch ready and he looked up and said, "For you, Mommy." At this she broke into tears and grabbed him in her arms. She was hugging him and kissing him and saying, "You brought your mother a flower, you brought your mother a flower, I love you so much, I love you so much."

Then I understood something else about God. Not only is it easy to offend him but it is very easy to please him. Because God loves each one of us more than that mother loved that child—much, much more. If it took so little by the child to make that mother cry with joy, it takes just as little to please God. It's dangerous to love because now you can get hurt very easily, but you can be pleased very easily too. And I learned that through that little Spanish baby boy and his mother in tears of joy over such a little thing as a faded flower in a dirty little hand.

MARIA DEL CARMEN

One day I went to visit a cloistered convent of Carmelite nuns outside Madrid where I wanted to say Mass. I noticed that there was something like a gravestone for a little girl whose body had been placed there. So I asked the nun through the grill about it. She said, "Her name was Maria del Carmen, and her family name was Gonzalez-Valerio. I'll give you a book on her life." I went home thinking, "I'm not sure I want to read this book because after all, the girl was nine years old when she died. She certainly couldn't have been bad." But I brought the book home and out of curiosity I began to look at it. The more I read the more I liked it, so I read the whole thing.

I went back to the convent later on and saw that this little girl had died in 1939 and had a sister who was a nun in that convent. Later on I met her brother who worked at the airport. He helped me out at the airport one day when I had a problem, so I got to know the family a little.

Maria lived in Madrid with her rather well-to-do family. Her father had been an officer in the army, though he had retired. But it was at the time of the civil war in Spain, a war of the rich, the powerful, and the Church against the students and the poor. Because Maria's father was on the right—the Franco side—the army from the left which had taken over Madrid came to get her father and eventually they shot him. Maria was around six years old when they shot her father. She had brothers and sisters, one younger, I think, and three or four older.

Instead of being angry with those who killed her father, she felt badly for them and thought she should pray for them so God would forgive them. Much of her life from then on was about how she wanted to pray for those who killed her father.

The mother and the children moved out of Madrid and moved to a safer area in San Sebastian in the north. One Christmas she took all her gifts, still wrapped, and brought them to the nuns at the school she attended to give to poor children. The nun asked her, "Don't you want to open them and see what you have?" And she said, "No, they'll have more fun opening the gifts themselves." There are other stories like this that made me think she was just a good little girl. But something else in her story made me think that she is truly a saint. In fact, she has already been declared "venerable" (a person who lived in a heroic way the virtues of faith, hope, and charity) by Pope John Paul II on January 16, 1996, which is the first step toward canonization.

On April 9, 1939, when she was nine years old, she went to the Church of the Good Shepherd in San Sebastian with her grandmother. It was Holy Week. After Communion her grandmother said she closed her eyes and knelt there deep in prayer, very deep into prayer, so much so that when Mass finished her grandmother did not want to interrupt her. She waited for her to finish. The grandmother said, "I waited and finally she opened her eyes, we got up and walked out of church and, as we got out of church the little girl said, 'Grandma, now you can buy me pastry.'" In Spain, you eat pastry on a very special day when you want to celebrate something. So her grandmother said, "Maria del Carmen, you're always making sacrifices and doing penance and here we are in Holy Week and you want to eat pastry?" And she said, "Yes, grandmother, today you can buy me pastry." Her grandmother never forgot that.

A few weeks later the little girl suddenly got very sick with a serious ear infection. While she was sick she said to her mother, "Mommy, Daddy died a martyr, and I'm going to die a victim." Now, a victim means someone who offers himself to God to suffer on behalf of others. They wondered where she got this idea. They think that she learned it from a former nun who had been her tutor. She got progressively worse, and in July she was in the hospital and in a very serious condition. On her aunt's wedding day, the 16th of July, the aunt brought flowers from the wedding to the hospital. The next day her mother came in and the little girl said, "Mommy, today I am going to die." Her mother said, "Don't say that." She said, "Well, Mommy, you ought to be happy. I'm going to go to heaven and see Daddy. If you have any errands for him, tell me and I'll tell him."

Then she added, "But first I have to go to confession." Her mother said, "Maria Carmen, you don't have any sins!" She said, "Oh yes, I do. I've got two." She said, "Yesterday, I didn't say my prayers." And her mother, "Yesterday you were suffering so much. You were so sick. How could you pray?"

"Well, I've got another one though," she said. "I didn't like the nurse."

Her mother said, "Well, the nurse was changing all your bandages and everything and it hurt you so much."

"I know, but she was doing it to help me and I didn't like her. So, Mommy, call her. I want to ask her to forgive me."

She insisted, so they called the nurse, who was still living when I was in Spain, and the little girl said, "Please forgive me. Yesterday when you changed my bandage, I didn't like you. Would you please forgive me?"

The nurse cried. Then she said, "Okay, Mommy, now please sing for me the song about Jesus." The title of the song in Spanish is *"Jesus, Mio, Que Bueno Eres,"* which means "My Jesus, how good you are."

She said, "Do you remember they sang that at my First Communion? Would you sing it again?" So her mother started singing. When she finished, the little girl said, "And now who's singing?" Her mother said, "Nobody." She said, "Oh yes, don't you hear that? Can't you hear that beautiful singing?" Just then her grandmother walked in and she said, "Grandma, who's singing? You can hear that can't you? Who's that singing?"

Her Grandmother didn't know what to say, so she said, "Maybe it's the angels." She said, "Oh that's what it is. They're coming to get me. Here they come." She raised her hands as though she were going to get up and fell back dead. But her body did not get cold. They put the flowers they had around her body on the bed and they said the next day those flowers were still very fresh while the ones that were in the water had faded. They even called the doctors and said, "Please, are you sure she died?" There was no heartbeat, no pulse, nothing. The doctors insisted she was dead.

Sometime later they found the notebook where she had kept notes. On the cover of the notebook it said in Spanish, *Privado, privado, privadisimo.* Which means "private, private, very private" or "personal, personal, very personal." So now, of course, since she had died they looked in it and they found that she had written the 9th of April 1939, "Today in the church of The Good Shepherd, I gave myself to God." The word she used in Spanish for "gave" was *entregar*, and there's no way to translate that to what it means in Spanish. The closest in English is "I gave myself." It means a complete, total gift of your whole self to God for anything He wants.

There's an expression in French that's hard to translate but it is something like "A saint who is sad is a sad saint." If you go around being sad, you're really a sad saint. It doesn't sound the same in English but I think you get the meaning. And, for a little girl of nine years old to make a complete gift of herself to God and to be so deep in prayer that her Grandmother couldn't even disturb her for a while, then come out and say, "Let's celebrate. Let's buy some pastry," during Holy Week is a remarkable thing. She didn't give the reason, but now we know. Now that we found that she had written that that was the day she had made a complete gift of herself to God and after that she knew she was going to suffer and die, but that it was okay. There are a lot of other things about her life but that's the one that convinced me that she had to be holy. There have been many favors that have been received through her intercession.

Whether or not we can prove that they were miracles and first-class miracles to get her beatified and canonized is another thing. For example, I remember reading in a book of her life about a certain man who was sick and dying and hadn't been to church for years and years. His daughter said, "Dad, could I call the priest?" He said, "No, I don't want to see any priest." So his daughter got a picture of this little girl, Maria del Carmen, who had already died, of course, and put it under her father's pillow without him knowing it. And the next morning when she came in he said, "Call a priest. I want to go to confession. I want to talk to a priest."

She said, "Last night you didn't want to. How come you want to now?" He said, "During the night this little girl appeared to me and she smiled and said, "Why don't you want to come to heaven with us? It's so nice. If you only knew how nice it is." And just then the picture fell off the bed and his daughter picked it up and he said, "What's that?" And she said, "Well, I put this picture under your pillow last night." He looked at the picture and said, "That's the girl! That's the girl! That's the girl that I saw." Of course, that's not the kind of miracle—if you want to call it a miracle—that Rome would accept to canonize anybody, but it's certainly a beautiful story.

I once went to see a young girl with very bad cancer in a hospital in Rhode Island. I brought a relic of Maria del Carmen and we prayed for this 12-year-old girl, and little by little she was healed. The last time I saw her she was about six feet tall playing basketball in high school and doing very, very well. Some might say, "How do we know it's not the treatment she got? How do we know it's the prayer?" We can't prove it, but that's one more thing that points to the power of prayer.

PRAYING FOR ANDY

I want to tell you about my nephew, Andy Maxfield, and his Muscular Dystrophy, the most severe and rapidly progressing form of that terrible disease. In 1974 when I understood that through the power of the Holy Spirit, we could do what Jesus empowered us to do: "to cure diseases ... and heal the sick," I started to do it and saw that people were being healed. Then I thought of Andy. He was about 11, and he had had muscular dystrophy since he was three years old. His parents were told that he had what is called Duchenne Muscular Dystrophy, so that he would get progressively worse and at 21, possibly a little more, he would pass away. At that time, there had been one recorded case of someone living to 26, which was a record.

He was getting progressively worse and at the age of 11, when all of this was happening with the Holy Spirit and me, he could only get around on crutches. I consulted a few people who were more into this ministry of healing and asked them about praying for Andy. They encouraged me, saying, "God can do anything. Don't ever think anything's impossible. But this kind of healing sometimes takes a lot of prayer, a lot of time."

So we started a prayer group before I went back to Spain. We agreed to pray twenty-four hours straight for him.

At 7:00 one evening I said Mass in the home of one of the prayer group members. And then we began to pray for Andy. Of course, it wasn't that we were mentioning his name continually, but we were praising God and at the same time asking God to heal him. His father brought him to us and we prayed with him, explaining to him that we just wanted to say a prayer for him. We didn't say much more because we didn't want to upset him. After this we sent him home. As the night wore on, some of us would rest while others kept on praying. But there was always somebody praying. And we kept up through the next day until 7:00 the next evening, when we had another Mass.

I was really convinced that something would happen, because you never pray in vain. God always listens to prayer, but I couldn't see that anything had happened. I finished the summer and went back to Spain and left Andy in God's hands.

In the years that followed he got progressively worse, but he also did very well in his studies with private tutors; he was quite intelligent. As he got older he began to draw and paint and later on sold some of his paintings and got very well known in Leominster. As he began using wheelchairs and electric wheelchairs, he rode around the city and got to know people and organized fund raisers for Muscular Dystrophy.

The years went by and he got to be in his late 20s, and then his early 30s. The doctors, who never expected him to live so long, were very surprised. But he got progressively worse and eventually at 40 years old he finally got to the point where he could not move at all. Then he got pneumonia, was on a ventilator to breathe, and finally had to be put on a feeding tube. Eventually, he himself asked if he could be taken off the machines and allowed to die. His family consulted doctors, priests, and one another and, finally, they all agreed.

Andy with me and my mother.

He spoke to the family one-by-one, thanked them and told them he loved them, was taken off the machines, and died. When we prayed for him 24 hours straight he was not healed in the way that we wanted him to be healed, so in a sense our prayers were not answered. But in a larger sense our prayers were, indeed, answered because God certainly gave us something through his life. His life span exceeded the doctors' expectations, but, more importantly his life, as God gave him the grace to live it, was a great source of strength and inspiration to many other people. There were some nice articles that came out and many letters to the editor in the newspaper about him when he died. So much came out of his life that no one would ever have expected. So I really believe our prayers *were* answered. I wanted to tell that story so that people would not think that God doesn't listen to prayers.

GOD IS LOVE

I wrote earlier about the vulnerability of God and how God loves so much. Of course, God is identified with love in many places in the Bible. But I learned this truth deeply in my heart little by little. God is love and, therefore, if God is love, then he has to love all the time because if he stopped loving then he would stop being what he is in his very essence. All we have to do is allow God to love us. He cannot force it on us because it is a free gift and we are free to reject it, as many people do. I would like to tell something that happened many years ago that relates to this.

In 1958, I went for a check-up at the Lahey Clinic in Boston and the doctor who was poking at the front of my neck said, "You have something here on your thyroid that needs to be removed." I said, "Well, I'll have to go home and talk with my Superiors. Maybe in a few weeks we could arrange ... " The doctor interrupted me and said, "No, this has to be done now."

This made me a little bit anxious to say the least. So I said, "I still have to go back home and talk with my Superiors about all this." They asked me to call soon to arrange for a bed at the hospital and for the surgery. Of course, my Superiors consented at once and so I arranged to go back in a day or so.

I had now been ordained three years. When I was first ordained I thought I was going to save the whole world by myself and I hadn't started yet. Now I was facing some kind of surgery that seemed rather serious, if not life-threatening. All of a sudden it dawned on me that the mother of one of the men who been ordained a priest with me had had surgery on her thyroid for a tumor and she died on the operating table. What with the sense of urgency the doctors seemed to have, all I could think of was, "Well, is this the end?" I was really anxious and I went into the hospital and began to think, "Here I am only in my late 20's, a priest only three years, maybe facing death." When I did die, what would happen to me then? Where would I go? I hope I would go to heaven but I've heard about purgatory and I've heard about hell. I think I would avoid that, I hope, but who knows. I don't know.

I was thinking about all this before they came to get me. All of a sudden I started thinking: "I've been telling everybody that God is love. God loves all the time. If God loves all the time, well this is his way of loving me. His way of loving me right now is through this. I can't understand why, why he would do it this way, but all I can say is, "Lord, I don't like this and I don't understand it, but if this is your way of loving me, with this surgery through any pain I might go through, through even dying and whatever happens after I die—as long as it's your way of loving me, then I will say right now, go ahead, Lord, love me. Just don't stop loving me and I know you won't. So thank you."

I suppose this was the kind of prayer we read in the Book of Psalms where the psalmist begins listing all his troubles and then trusting God and placing himself in God's hands. In any event, right there I was filled with so much peace. They came to get me and said it was time to go to the operating room. I remember them wheeling me into the operating room. I had closed my eyes. I heard somebody say, "This guy's asleep already." And I thought I don't care what happens; I'm in God's hands and God loves me and everything that's going to happen he is going to love me through it and he's never going to stop loving me and I'm so happy. God loves me right now and is not ever, ever going to stop loving me. I felt so much at peace that I felt almost like I would die, because I felt so ready to meet God who loves me and into whose hands I had surrendered completely. I had abandoned myself completely into God's hands and I knew I was in good hands and it didn't make any difference what happened, even if I died. I almost looked forward to dying.

Later when it was all over and I woke up they told me that what they removed from my thyroid had been cancerous. It was cancer cells that had not begun to spread yet. I never forgot that experience and sometimes I share it with others because I think it's a good experience for people to know about. It is so important that you simply abandon yourself into God's hands and really believe that no matter what happens he will never stop loving you. God cannot stop loving you because God *is* love, so it is not in his nature ever to stop loving. As St. Paul says in his letter to the Romans, nothing can separate us from the love of God in Jesus Christ, not even death.[26]

TOWARD THE LIGHT

I know many people are interested in knowing more about near-death experiences. I would like to tell about two that I know of personally that I think can be helpful. The first concerns a good friend of mine, somebody I went to school with. We were in grammar school and high school together until I went to the seminary and I've been in touch with her and her husband and her family for several years now. Some years back she had to have some very serious surgery and during the surgery her heart stopped and she died. The doctors walked out and said to the nurses, "Get the body ready for the morgue." But one of her doctors went back and he told her later, "I started working on you and, all of a sudden we got a heartbeat and you started breathing and you came back."

She told me that in the time that she was gone, she saw herself floating away and entering a kind of light—a very, very bright light, brighter than any light she had ever seen. She said she was going toward the light, and the closer she got the more peaceful and joyful she felt. It was the most beautiful experience she had ever had. She said that all of a sudden she saw her grandmother, who had died years earlier, coming toward her. And she came up to her and said, "No, it's not time yet. You have to go back, but always remember that to cry is to pray, or if you wish, tears are prayers; and now go back."

---

[26] Romans 8:31-39.

She said she didn't want to come back here and added, "I will never again be afraid to die."

Then she asked me, "Why would my grandmother say, she said it in French by the way, 'To cry is to pray?'" I said, "Please understand that every one of your tears is a prayer. Praying is not just with words. God doesn't need words. We're never going to find words to impress God. We do the best we can but when you believe in God and you cry, hoping and expecting him to have pity on you and your family and come to you; those are prayers. I think that's what your grandmother meant."[27] I like to share that because I think that it is meaningful and that was a near-death experience where I know the person very well.

The other near death experience that I know of quite well happened here at the Dartmouth-Hitchcock Medical Center when I was working as Chaplain years ago. I had gone to see a patient who had come in for heart catheterization. Later that day when he was leaving the hospital to go home he suddenly collapsed and his heart stopped. They called a "code blue" and began to work on him and they called me too, as Chaplain, to come. They finally got his heart beating again. I didn't see him until the next day and he said he knew what had happened and he said in that time, "I saw myself floating away from myself. I don't know how to say this but it was like I was down there but I was floating away and I had an angel on each side of me and we were going up higher and higher and I was peaceful and happy and joyful. All of a sudden they put those paddles on me and shocked me." He said, "I felt like I got hit by a truck and I guess my heart started up." But he said, "I will never again be afraid to die." He told me that himself.

I don't want to draw too many conclusions from this, about what death is all about, but what I do want to say is that, if God is love, our first meeting after we die has to be some kind of a meeting with God. I'm not surprised that people have these beautiful experiences. We're not made for this life.

---

[27] See Romans 8:26-27.

We're made for something more than this. And so when we first meet that "more," I'm not surprised that it's a good experience. That's all I think we can draw from these two stories.

OUR LADY OF LA SALETTE

I want to say something about Our Lady of La Salette because the order to which I belong is dedicated to her and she is so important to me. La Salette is a town in the French Alps where the Virgin Mary appeared to two children on September 19, 1846. At the time she appeared she was crying and asking people to come back to God. She cried all the time that she spoke to the children. She never stopped crying until the last moment she went up to heaven. It's a very special apparition, I think, because the tears of Mary show us the concern of God for the world. Mary did not "escape" from heaven and come to tell us a few secrets about what we should be doing. Instead, it was  God allowing us to understand how Jesus had suffered for us. As a matter of fact, the children kept repeating that what was brightest and most beautiful about the apparition was the crucifix, the cross that she wore, and Jesus seemed to be alive on the cross, and they couldn't take their eyes from him.

La Salette is an apparition that brings many people back to God. Lourdes is an apparition where many people are healed and I think people are brought to God there also. And people are healed at La Salette. But, I think the biggest graces or gifts from God—not to call them miracles—are people coming back to God through this apparition of Our Lady of La Salette in tears. I've heard more than once that almost every

La Salette missionary priest could tell a story about some conversion associated with Our Lady of La Salette that he has heard about in the confessional. Jacques Maritain (1882-1973), one of the greatest Christian philosophers of the last 100 years, and invited by Pope Paul VI to the Second Vatican Council, and his wife, Raïssa, were both converted and baptized at La Salette in 1906. They had become atheists at the Sorbonne in Paris.

I just want to tell of one conversion in my own particular ministry that I attribute to the tears of Mary. Nobody likes to see his or her mother cry. I think when your mother cries for you, it does something to you. In any case, one day I was sitting in the confessional in Attleboro. All of a sudden I heard some steps and somebody walked in. Now the person who came in for confession, whoever came in, could either kneel behind the screen, where I could not see the person, or could come around and sit in a chair in front of me. So, this man came around the screen and just stood there and looked down at me sitting there and said, "What am I doing here?" I said, "I don't know; why are you asking?" He said, "Because I drive by this Shrine every day on my way to work. I've been doing that for years and I have never stopped here at the Shrine. Never." And he said, "Just now, my car drove in here alone. I mean, I don't remember turning the wheel. The first thing I knew my car was in here and I was parked and now I'm in here with you. What is this, a confessional?" I said, "Yes. Would you like to go to confession?" He said, "Me?" And I don't remember if he said it had been 20 years or 30 years, but whatever it was, it was many years but I said, "That's no problem. It doesn't matter how long it's been." And he said, "Okay."

So he sat down and we talked for quite a while and he confessed his whole life. I got up to lay my hands on his head and gave him an absolution and blessing and he got up crying, tears in his eyes, threw his arms around me and said, "Father, I don't know what I am doing here. I don't know how I got here. All I know is that this is the most beautiful day of my life."

That's La Salette; that's Our Lady of La Salette and her tears. They'll do that to people.

INTIMACY WITH THE LORD

When we began a prayer group in my hometown, a young girl—maybe 14 or 15—showed up on the first night. One of the people there who had quite a gift of discernment told me later, "Keep your eyes on that young girl. She is going to be very special. I kept thinking while we were praying '... and a little child shall lead them.'"[28]

As the years went by whenever I would come home from Spain, this girl would show up at the prayer group. She seemed to me and to others a model of prayer. You could tell she knew how to pray and there was just a beautiful, faith-filled simplicity about her. I began to hear very good things about her from many people. Eventually I heard she had married and when I would come back home I would see her occasionally. She had a great gift of discernment and prophecy. For example, she called her mother one morning and said, "Mom, be very careful when you go to work today." Her mother, knowing her, was extra careful and was able to avoid a near accident. One day, when I had come home I took my friend, Fr. Joe Mahoney to meet her. When we arrived and went into her house her children were playing on the floor; I think there were two of them. We sat down at the kitchen table, and knowing already from past experiences and conversations with her how close she was to God, I said, "Tell us, how are things going with life with the Lord?" She's very humble and we could see that the question embarrassed her and this made her hesitate. I said, "It would be nice if you shared anything with us that you think might be helpful."

---

[28] Isaiah 11:6.

So little by little we were able to draw her out. She began by saying, "I know the Lord loves me very much and I love him and, you know, it's gotten so it's like he courts me. I don't know just how to explain that, but I feel as though he's courting me. For example, if I know my husband is coming home, maybe I'll go and comb my hair and try to fix myself up a little bit because I know my husband will be home any moment. And I can almost hear the Lord say, "That's good, do that, but do it for me, too. It's like he wants me to do everything for him."

She seemed so shy about telling us, almost like she shouldn't be saying these things. Then she said, "Sometimes he lets me feel the way he feels." And she added, "Sometimes that is so beautiful. Sometimes it's very difficult." She said, "Because the thing that makes him suffer the most is our rejection of his love. We don't really believe or we don't care that he loves us and so we go about our business as though it makes no difference. He's offering us so much. It's almost as though we don't care and we don't want what he's offering. And that's what hurts him the most. It hurts so much."

She continued, "One day he allowed me to feel all that was hurting him—the rejection of his love by so many people. It got so bad that after a couple of days I had to ask him, 'Please, Lord, I can't take anymore. I have a lot of things to do for my husband and my children and would you please back off a little because it's gotten so that it is so heavy on me I can hardly take it.' So he left me with a little more peace for a while."

Our conversation went on like this for a while. As we walked out of the house and got into the car Fr. Mahoney said to me, "Leo, she is for real. She is for real." And he added, "Boy, would I like to sit her down in front of all the priests I know and say, 'You guys listen to this girl!' I don't think I've ever met anybody as close to God as she seems to be."

I like to share this story because I want people to know that this kind of relationship with Christ is possible in life. It is possible to have that kind of friendship with the Lord.

He wants her to be a good wife and mother. He lets her know that, but also expects that everything she would do for them she would also do for him. I think we need to know that.

HE AND I

I would like to share a few thoughts about a book called *He and I* by Gabrielle Bossis (1874-1950).[29] Bossis was a French stage actress who recorded her conversations (interior locutions) with Jesus over a span of 14 years. She had a spiritual director who was a Jesuit priest. One day she showed him all these things she was writing down and he said, "Oh, this has to be from God, and we need to publish it." She didn't want to, but he insisted and then she said, "Well, you may if you wish, but without my name. Do not give my name." So it was first published in France without her name, with permission from her bishop, who also thought it was from the Lord. After she died it was published in her name.

When I began to read it I wanted to be convinced that this is from God. After all, anybody can say, "I'm hearing a voice." The more I read, the more I thought, "Yes, this probably is from God." I'm now very convinced. It doesn't mean that every single word in the book is from God. So many of the thoughts and so much of the book really seem to me to be from God. Some of the thoughts are so beautiful that I wanted to share at least a couple of these now.

One day Jesus said to Gabrielle, "Is it because I'm God that you think I don't need tenderness? Please be tender to me." Another day he says something to her like, "Time is not enough for me to love you. I need eternity. I will love you through eternity because time is not enough."

Of course, he was asking her to pray all the time, so she did pray. One day she was waiting for the train in Lyons in France. She began to pray in silence and eventually she heard

---

[29] Sherbrooke, Quebec: Médiaspaul, 1985.

the voice. Gabrielle often would say she could tell by the tone of the voice how he felt. She said this time he was very sad. He said, "You know, Gabrielle, you're the only one thinking of me right now in this train station." She said, "I could tell that there was sadness in his voice."

One of the things the Lord made her understand was that he wanted to live again on Earth but only in us and through us. This is why we need to be one with Jesus and to allow him to live through us. Some people never allow him to really do that. To do so would be a loving response to Christ. A loving response would be to agree to have him live in us and use everything in our lives. He told Gabrielle he would use every beat of her heart, every breath she would take, every step she would take, if she wanted to, but it was up to her because we are free.

I want to come to some of the thoughts He gave Gabrielle about how she could help him save the world, and how she could offer him anything at all. One day she was doing some little thing and said, "Oh, Lord, you want me to offer even this!" Please remember that this woman never had any visions or apparitions. It was just a voice that she heard which was judged by many intelligent people to be the voice of the Lord. And, the voice said to her, "Yes, even that, because I collect atoms. I collect the dust of time."

Another time she was walking upstairs and offering each step to Jesus and then paused and said, "How could you ever accept such tiny things?" And the voice said, "You call them tiny, yet you just used your memory, your understanding, your will, your entire being, to give to me out of love. I don't think that's tiny." If only we could understand that we could and should live our lives in union with Jesus and then everything becomes worth so much. Everything takes on a new value. To save not only the people we love, but the whole world. That's his plan. We are part of his body, part of the mystical body of Christ.

One day she came home from church and her feet were very cold and she said, "Lord, I offer you my two cold feet to save two souls." And she heard the voice say, "Two or two thousand. I could save two. I could save two thousand. After all, I'm God. I can do what I want. But, yes, I will take and use your two cold feet. Give them to me. I will use them."

On another day the voice said to her, "If only you could help me save everyone in your time, while you are on Earth. Maybe this sounds like a lot, but remember, love is daring. If you really love me, why don't you desire to give me all of humanity as though this were in your power? Why don't you dare to say to me, 'Lord, I want you to save everybody.' I would like it if you said that. You should be daring. Take a chance. If you love me, then dare. Dare me to save the whole world."

Another thought I liked is when he said, "Offer me all the crosses in the world right now. There are so many." It was 1943 during the war. "There are so many crosses right now. So few people think of offering them to me. Don't let anything be lost." It's not that we have to believe that it would be lost if it were not offered, but that certainly it would be worth a lot more if it were offered, especially out of love. And at least we who believe should take our part in the body of Christ and offer it up.

These are some of the special thoughts I remember from *He and I*, but let me finish with something I have never forgotten that I read in a book of prayer by Simon Tugwell, an English Dominican, who is a convert to the Catholic faith.[30] He was one of my professors in Rome when I was there. He writes about how the Lord appeared to St. Catherine of Siena one day and said, "Catherine, there are some souls that are going to be lost unless you pray for them, and you sacrifice for them. I could save them without you but that's not my plan. Because you're my bride, because you're one with me, I need you to help me save them." So Catherine began to pray and offer some sacrifices for these souls that he had spoken of.

---

[30] *Prayer: Living With God*, Springfield, Illinois: Templegate Publishers, 1980.

Some time later, the Lord appeared and said, "Catherine, they've been saved." He said, "With your prayers and your sacrifices you conquered me. You won." And he said, "I'm so glad you won, because I didn't want them to be lost." So you see again, always with Jesus, through him and with him, we have this great power, out of love, to offer him everything we have so that he can live in us. By looking at the lives of the saints and holy people and reading books like *He and I*, we can learn how the Lord counts on each of us to be a member of his body and help him save the world.

THE POWER OF EVIL AND THE GREATER POWER OF GOD

There are things I wish to say now that are difficult to write about and even more difficult to read. I had doubts and hesitations about writing these things, but after speaking with a few friends, I have become convinced that what I have to say may be helpful, especially to priests. The point I want to make is that in the name of Jesus Christ we have power over all kinds of evil. So I am going to be telling about Satan and evil spirits and I want to warn anyone who is frightened by something like this that perhaps you might not want to read this.

Pope Paul VI, several years ago, said very clearly, "We need to understand that there is such a thing as a devil, and there is more than one." There *are* evil spirits; we've always believed that and we should understand that.

I never expected, of course, to ever get into this kind of ministry, but after I got involved in what is called Charismatic Renewal, I had a chance to attend a week-long Charismatic convention for priests at Steubenville University in Ohio. We must have been a thousand priests and ten or twelve bishops. One night Fr. Francis McNutt, who was well known in the healing ministry, gave a talk on healing. At the end of his talk he said, "I would like to say a prayer right now over everybody, asking God's healing for all of us." So he said a prayer and then he said, "Now, because the most powerful prayer is to praise God, let's all of us begin to praise God, in our own way."

We were all in a huge tent, where they had set up rows and rows of chairs, and he was up on a stage with a microphone. So everybody began to praise God out loud in any words they wanted:

"Alleluia!"

"We praise you, Lord!"

"We love you, Lord!"

It was very impressive to see all these priests praising God as we will all do in heaven someday. We were not asking anything now but just praising God with all the saints and angels in heaven. I've learned, over the years, that this is a powerful prayer because you're concentrating only on God and not on your own needs and desires. You're not concentrating on yourself or anyone else or asking God what to do, but instead you are just saying he is great and he deserves praise and glory.

As we were praising God, and glorifying God in this way, all of a sudden, several rows behind me, we heard terrible screams. I have never heard that kind of scream before—it was bone-chilling and unearthly and very, very loud. It was also very frightening, I don't mind telling you. So everybody stopped and turned around and we saw that one of the priests had fallen to the ground and he was the one who was screaming. I couldn't see him very well with all the priests around me, but I got the impression that he was not aware of what was going on.

Fr. McNutt, who was still up at the podium, very calmly said, "Let's just pray for our brother priest now. Everybody raise their right hand toward this priest on the ground." Fr. McNutt began to say; "In the name of Jesus Christ I command any spirit that might be bothering my brother priest to be gone, to leave him alone."

At this, we all put our right hand out and began to pray for our brother priest. After a couple of minutes, the screaming stopped and the priest stood up. He looked around rather surprised and seemed to wonder what had happened. Fr. McNutt began to say, "We thank you, Jesus. We thank you, God." Then everything finished and we walked out of the tent.

Of course, after the meeting everybody was talking about this and wondering, "What was that all about?" And then most of the priests went to the chapel where the Blessed Sacrament was exposed and where there would be some singing and prayers before the end of the day. Although I usually went, this night I had to make a phone call and I only learned what happened later from those who were there.

They began to pray in front of the Blessed Sacrament and this same man who had fallen in the tent suddenly fell and began screaming again. A bishop who was there took a crucifix and went close to this priest and said, "In the name of Jesus Christ I command any evil spirits to be gone." But the screams continued. He then said, "I command you in the name of Jesus Christ, tell me who you are." And a voice screamed, "Pride." The bishop said, "In the name of Jesus Christ I command any spirit of pride to be gone from my brother priest." All of a sudden the priest got up again looking bewildered, wondering what had happened to him.

Then the afflicted priest fell and started screaming all over again. This time the bishop asked, "Tell me your name." The voice said, "Lust." The bishop again said, "In the name of Jesus Christ I command the spirit of lust to be gone." A few minutes later he got up and seemed to be okay, and then a third time he went down and began to scream and roll around on the floor. So the bishop asked again, "Tell me who you are in the name of Jesus Christ." And the voice said, "Evil." The bishop said, "In the name of Jesus Christ I command the spirit of evil to be gone."

And then, as told to me by a priest who was there, "It was like a hot wind that flew right up the aisle." The priest got up and everything was all right. So the bishop said, "Okay, let's continue to pray and praise God."

Well, you can imagine when everybody came out of the chapel what the topic of conversation was. As I drove back to Washington, D.C., on the weekend with three or four other priests that's all we could talk about. I remember one priest saying, "Gosh, I wasn't sure if I believed in evil spirits before but I sure do now." Everyone was saying, "We know now what power there is in the name of Jesus Christ."

Less than a week later I was back in my hometown. My friend, Fr. Mahoney told me he was having a weekend retreat with Spanish-speaking people and asked me to come and assist him with some talks, prayers and so forth. So Friday evening we began and Bishop Timothy Harrington from Worcester was there. The Bishop said the Mass, but he did not speak Spanish. So he said to me, "I'll give the homily and you translate for me." We did that and when he finished he turned to me and said, "Do you think these people would like to be prayed over?" And I said, "Oh, yes."

He said to the people, "If you'd like to come around the altar rail, we'll pray." So he stretched out his hands and began to pray for the people. There were Fr. Mahoney and myself and a young priest who had just been ordained from the Boston area. We were standing at different spots in the sanctuary near the people. All of sudden in front of the young priest a woman fell to the floor and began rolling around and making some strange noises.

I went right over put my hand out and said, "Look, just do what I'm going to do. In the name of Jesus Christ I command any spirit here that is not of God to be gone." And right away the woman got up and looked around seeming a bit confused about what had just happened. And then others began to fall. So we kept saying prayers for those who were afflicted and finally all that stopped and we continued the Mass.

I still remember when we went into the sacristy my friend Fr. Mahoney, who has quite a sense of humor, turned to the Bishop and said, "Well, Bishop, that was quite a ballgame wasn't it?" And the Bishop turned to me and said, "Ballgame? What was going on out there?" I said, "Well, I'm not sure."

I found out later that all of the people at the Mass who had been falling down had attended "spiritism" meetings at which somebody would conjure up the spirits of relatives who had died to talk to them. Of course, that's forbidden by the Church. They didn't realize that they shouldn't be doing this but it seems, from what I've heard, that they thought it was okay.

The next day Fr. Mahoney and I and the other priest gave some talks, led some prayers and had a Mass and there were a few people who manifested some strange behavior. We prayed with them and everything seemed to be okay. Then Sunday came and we were having the last Eucharist on Sunday afternoon; I was saying the Mass. At one point we began to pray that the Holy Spirit would come in the name of Jesus Christ to make us all holy. There was a young black girl there and she was standing maybe ten feet away from the holy table and holding another young girl by the arm. All of a sudden this girl screamed and just flew through the air, right under the table where I was saying Mass. She literally didn't touch the floor until she got under the table. The other girl fell down and was able to let go. The black girl was there rolling around on the floor. So we said some prayers in the name of Jesus Christ and then she calmed down and seemed to be fine. Once again, the powerful name of Jesus Christ drove the evil one away.

Father Mahoney and I were so intrigued with this whole subject of evil spirits, which was so new to us, that we both decided to attend a workshop on the subject on Long Island. It was a weeklong program and there were about 100 priests and one or two bishops. One of the things I was made to understand, which I suppose I had simply overlooked in my previous theological studies, is that there is such a thing as evil spirits (which we may call Satan or the devil), and that they have different ways of bothering us.[31] In order to understand this we should think of a fortress. Think of a person as the fortress and sometimes the enemy, in this case the evil spirit, is outside the fortress shooting arrows which are temptations. You want to find a way to avoid these temptations. Sometimes the enemy—Satan, evil spirits—gets closer and perhaps begins to pound on the doors or walls, hoping to get in. This is what is called an oppression. Now, we must not see everything I'm going to describe later as an oppression by evil spirits, but it can be. For example, why is it some days I have no patience or some days I have no joy? For some reason I can't be happy or I seem to lose my faith. Well, these *might* be oppressions where an evil spirit is bothering us.

There is a simple, straightforward remedy for oppressions when we are aware of them. We can just say, "In the name of Jesus Christ, leave me alone. Come, Holy Spirit, and give me the faith, the joy, the patience, the love, whatever I need." And usually that's enough.

Oppressions can occur not only to a person but can happen to a place or a whole community. At the workshop we learned about an Episcopal parish where people were wondering why they didn't feel like praying there. There didn't seem to be a lot of joy there. Finally, the Episcopal priest consulted somebody who knew about the power of evil spirits. So they prayed and commanded any evil spirits that might be bothering their parish to be gone and the priest said that later on people were coming to church and saying, "Did you change something around here? Are these new carpets, or have the walls been painted? Something is different. It is so nice to come here now."

---

[31] The words of the well-known hymn by Martin Luther, "A Mighty Fortress Is Our God," which is found in many Catholic hymnals, describe Satan's power over humanity being overcome by the name of Jesus Christ. So we need to understand that this is all part of orthodox Christianity and the reason we do not hear very much about it is that it is frightening and unpleasant to think about.

However, sometimes the enemy manages to breach the walls of the fortress and get inside and control one little corner or one little room. This is, of course, a little more complicated because now he's into your life in a more direct way. This is what is called, for lack of a better word, an obsession. So we have temptations, oppressions and now obsessions. The final, most extreme, stage is when the enemy controls the whole fortress and that is called a possession. I have never seen anything like an actual possession, which is quite rare, but I know that it has happened.

After the workshop Father Mahoney and I went to Leominster and later I went back to Spain. Back in Spain I had other experiences of the power of Satan or evil spirits that I want to relate to you. I can't be sure in every instance if these cases were oppressions or obsessions. In some cases I think I do know, but in any event we're speaking about more than just temptations now. And I do want to be clear that none of the examples that follow are about possessions.

I'll begin with rather minor examples. One day I was praying with people to be healed of physical sicknesses and a girl fell on the floor and was rolling around and making very strange noises. Of course, everybody was frightened. I said a prayer in silence so as not to frighten anyone and at first nothing happened, so I silently said, "In the name of Jesus Christ ..." All of a sudden she was okay. She got up and I noticed around her neck that she had a chain with one of those Italian horns on it. I asked her, "What is that?" And she said, "My boyfriend gave me that. It brings you good luck." One of the things I had learned in that workshop was that if the devil bothers you through oppression or obsession, it is usually because something has been adored, a window has been let open for him to get some power. One way that this can happen is through superstitions. If, for example, you start playing with Ouija boards, and begin to get serious about what you think it can do, you can open a window to evil sprits. I'm just trying to say that it is a possibility—a *possibility*—that, because you're putting your faith in something which is not of

God, you open a pathway for the devil to invade the fortress of your spiritual life. Our faith should be only in God and in the power of God. When we put our faith in anything else, whether it's a Ouija board or Italian horn, things can go wrong. In any case, I asked her to get rid of that horn and not to think that this was going to bring her any good luck. I suggested that she might like to replace the horn with a little cross and she readily agreed.

Another time I was asked to pray for a young girl who kept running away from home. Her mother, of course, was very worried about her. She said, "I don't know what's going on. Would you pray for her?" I said, "I'll ask her if she would mind." The girl was a little reluctant but she agreed. I began to pray for her and I had my hands on the girl's head. As her mother put her hand on the girl's shoulder the girl began to act in a very strange way. She began to writhe and move around and seemed to be frightened. I thought that was strange. So I took the mother's hand off her shoulder and immediately the girl calmed down. Then I said to the girl, "You go sit on the other side." I asked her mother to sit down. So I began to pray over the mother and all of a sudden she began to act in very strange ways and move around, writhing, and making strange sounds. So I began to think there maybe was something more going on here. So in silence I commanded any evil spirits that might be bothering her to be gone in the name of Jesus Christ. But nothing happened. Then I noticed she had a chain around her neck and I asked her, "What is this that you're wearing?" She said, "My horoscope." I said, "Would you mind taking it off." She took it off and immediately everything went well and she was fine. I said, "I think you'd better get rid of this. This is not good. Get yourself a cross or a holy medal. But I wouldn't wear this anymore."

Now, I don't want to imply that every time people believe in horoscopes, they're going to be bothered by the devil. I don't mean that. All I mean is that it can be an opening because you're putting your faith in something which is not of God. And that's never a good thing to do from a spiritual point of view. Such a practice can weaken us spiritually and make us susceptible to the powers of evil.

The Italian horn was at St. Bernard's Church in Fitchburg, Massachusetts and the horoscope was at St. Leo's Church in Leominster and what I'm going to tell now was at St. Ann's Church, also in Leominster. I was conducting a healing service, and at the end of the Mass people were coming up to be prayed over. I was going from person to person saying a prayer for healing. Two young women who were sisters and in their late 20s or early 30s came up. I began to pray and they both fell to the floor and they were rolling around and making sounds. In silence, I began to pray in the name of Jesus Christ. I commanded any evil spirit that might be bothering these women to be gone. Then they both got up looking at me in a puzzled way as if to say "What was that all about?" And I just said, "Okay, just praise God now and thank God. He loves you very much."

The following week I went back and again after Mass asked if anyone would like to come forward for a healing prayer. And again both the girls came up but this time only one girl fell. The other one didn't. So I said the prayer and she was all right, but this time her sister had seen what had happened. She told her sister, "You know, you were on the ground and rolling around and making strange sounds." So later that week the one who fell came to see me and said, "Could you tell me what happened the other night? My sister said I fell." So we sat down and I said, "Tell me a little bit about yourself." I began to ask a few questions about family and her faith. Did she go to church? Did she pray? Things like that. Finally, I said, "I'm not sure what to say to you but may I ask, have you been involved in anything superstitious in any way that you know of?" And she said, "I often see this woman who tells fortunes with a crystal ball." I said, "Really, why would you do that?" She said, "I'm interested in knowing what might happen." And she said, "She's really good; a lot of things she tells me actually happen." I said, "I don't doubt that at all, but now you tell me, where does she get her power?" And she said, "I don't know.

Where?" I said, "Well, it's not from God, because God doesn't work through glass balls and telling people fortunes and things like that." I quickly added, "I'm not accusing her of anything because I don't know what her motives are, but this is not good. You're putting your faith in someone and something which is not of God. you need to tell God you're sorry about that. I'm not accusing you of sin because you don't seem to realize that this is wrong, but it was wrong and so please tell God you're sorry that you put your faith in something like that and make up your mind that you will not go back anymore." She agreed and we prayed together about that and then I said a prayer over her and she was a completely changed person after that.

I want to emphasize at this point that I do not believe that you have to be a priest in order to cast out evil spirits. I do think that a priest has a special vocation and power to do this through his ordination and becoming in some sense another Christ, a representative of Christ on Earth. I think a priest does have a special power. But I also think that any Christian in the name of Jesus Christ can drive evil away.

There is no way that I could remember all the cases and all the people I was involved with in this kind of ministry but I'd like to give a case where I think I saw an obsession when I was in Spain. One day a priest who had become a good friend came to see me and asked to talk. So we sat down and he said, "Look, you don't know this but I'm gay." He said, "You don't know what a cross this is for me. I don't want to be this way. I just don't want to be this way." He added, "If I don't go looking for a man once a month at least, I'm just not at peace. And if I *do* go looking for a man once a month I'm not at peace either." And he said, "Can you help me?" This was not the first time I had dealt with somebody with this problem. But I don't think anyone had ever put it so clearly about how helpless he felt and how much he wanted to be free.

We spoke for a few minutes and I encouraged him and tried to make him understand that I didn't think he was bad or evil. I knew the great work he was doing and how much people loved him and I did the best I could to encourage him. Finally I said, "I don't know what else to tell you except that I would like to say a prayer with you if you don't mind." He said, "Of course, I don't mind." I got up and put my hands on his head and began to pray and, in silence, I said, "In the name of Jesus Christ I command any spirit of homosexuality that might be bothering my brother priest here to be gone from him right now. Jesus Christ is Lord. And I ask the Holy Spirit to fill him and give him new power."

About a month later I ran into him and he said, "What did you do to me?" I said, "What do you mean?" He said, "That day I went to see you and you prayed with me. What did you do?" I said, "I just prayed for you, that's all." He said, "Well, since that day not only have I not fallen into homosexuality, I can't. I can't." He added, "I feel like I'm in a suit of armor. I'm protected." I just replied, "God is good."

I didn't tell him what I had prayed for, how I had prayed. I just said, "God's good. I'm glad that you feel that way. Just praise God." Now I don't know what happened after that. And, in no way do I want to imply here that everybody who is homosexual is being controlled by Satan or evil spirits. There is so much about homosexuality that I don't understand and I don't mean to accuse anybody of anything. I do believe that homosexuality, like cancer, like death, was not part of God's original plan. Any kind of evil—not necessarily moral evil or guilt—came as a result of the fact that Satan got some power over this world and led us away from God.

Here's another example of the power of evil and the greater power of God. One day I was speaking to a very good nun whom I knew quite well. She was a very good, very holy person, doing great work, and was loved by everybody; just a wonderful person. She said, "I want to consult you. You know me, but you don't know everything about me."

She went on, "I have a problem and that is I have these horrible thoughts that go through my mind that have to do with sex. I keep getting these horrible pictures and thoughts

I AM THE HOLY LAND ... *and so are you*

going through my head. I don't know what to do about it." I said, "I hope you realize that that can happen to anybody and that's not a sin." She said, "I know but, please, every time I speak to a priest and mention this they say, 'Oh, don't you worry about that.' But you don't realize what a problem this is for me."

The more she spoke the more I realized that this was not quite normal. She kept telling me, "You don't understand. It just keeps coming and coming and coming and I just can't get rid of it." So I began to wonder whether there might be something sinister, something evil going on. So we talked and I tried to encourage her as much as possible and then finally I said, "Well, let's pray."

She was sitting in a chair across from me in this rather small parlor, maybe six or eight feet between us. I put my hands on my knees and I closed my eyes. I can clearly remember praying, "Heavenly Father, I pray in Jesus' name. And I have to tell you Father, that I don't know what I'm praying for and I don't know what to ask you. I don't understand this problem. I only know that I have a sister here who is suffering and I would like to help her and I ask you, Father, in Jesus' name to please help her."

I still had my eyes closed when all of a sudden, I thought I saw a large, dark figure bent over and heading toward the door. So I opened my eyes and there was nothing. So I thought to myself, "Maybe she swung her hand across and blocked the light off somehow from me and I just saw a shadow." But then I thought, "That would be strange because the light is up there and she's over there but maybe it was something like that." So I closed my eyes again and I kept on praying.

When I finished I didn't know what else to say in my prayer or to say to her so I said, "Sister, if you like we can talk again some other day and pray again. May I ask you though, have you noticed anything?" She said, "What do you mean?" I said, "Well, sometimes during prayer a person gets a certain idea, a certain feeling that things are better. Sometimes God speaks to us like that, with our thoughts, imaginings, or feelings. He's letting us know that he's with us."

She said, "No, nothing happened like that." And then, after hesitating a moment, she said, "Well, yeah, something odd did happen. When you were praying, all of a sudden I saw a black figure bent over and heading toward the door." I said, "Oh?" She said, "I thought maybe you had swung your hand across the light and I saw a shadow, but I opened my eyes and you were just sitting there with your eyes closed and you weren't moving."

I had noticed the same things when I had opened my eyes; she was just sitting there, not moving, with her eyes closed. So I said, "Sister, the reason I asked you is that I saw the same thing." And I said, "Let's just thank God now and praise him for what he is doing and for what he has done." And after that she was not bothered anymore.

REYNA

One day in the late 1970s I went to Burgos, a large city north of Valladolid where I was living in Spain, to give a weekend retreat to a prayer group. The priest who was directing this group asked me to speak to a woman who had come to see him with a problem that puzzled him. He said, "She's a rather elderly lady and I just don't understand, but somehow there is something very strange going on in her life." So I went to the hall and I began to give my talk to the group. A few minutes into my talk the door opened and in walked an elderly lady, at least 80 years old. She walked down to take a chair where I could see her quite well. Somehow I knew right away that she was the one the priest asked me to see. Just looking at her face I said to myself, "There's the lady with the problem."

When we finished and it was time for me to speak with this woman I asked the priest to come with me and to bring along a couple of women to join us. I did this because already I suspected there was something odd going on just by looking at her. I just knew I did not want to be alone with her.

He got two very mature women, very good Christians, to come and we went to a small room and sat down. I purposely sat the two women on either side of the elderly woman. The other priest and I sat facing her in chairs. We started with a prayer and then I addressed the elderly woman saying, "Father tells me you have some kind of a problem." And she said, "Yes. Every time I open my mouth to begin to pray I begin to curse God. Instead of praying I'm cursing God."

My first thought when I hear something like that is whether the person is sane or not. I wondered if she might have some psychological problem that I don't understand. So, I said, "Is that right. How long has this been going on?" She said, "For a few years now." I said, "Well, have you ever spoken to any other priests about it?" She said, "Oh, yes, but they always tell me the same thing, 'Oh, don't worry about that. You're not guilty of anything. That's no sin. I don't know what it is all about but you shouldn't think you're committing any sin.'" She added, "They always tell me the same thing but you don't understand, this is really bothersome."

I said, "Okay, we can talk about that but first of all would you mind if I ask you a few questions?" She said, "No, no." I said, "Your name again?" And she told me. "Have you always lived here?" "Where were you born?" She was answering my questions when all of a sudden she said, "Wait a minute. I know what you're getting at." She said, "You want to know all about me. You tell these two women to leave here."

Now I wasn't exactly sure what to do and so I called the two women out of the room with me and said, "You stay right here near the door, and you pray. I'll call you when I'm ready." I went back in and sat down with the priest and she said, "All right. I know you want to know all about me, so I'm going to tell you." She said, "I have committed just about every sin you can think of. For example, when it comes to sex, everything you can think of." And then she named a couple of sexual sins and said, "I never did that." And she said she had tried to kill her husband by poisoning him, though he survived. I asked her if there was anything else I should know. She said, "No, I think that's it."

I then went back outside to the two women and I said, "Okay, you can come back in." One of them said, "Wait a moment. While we were praying I got this strong, strong feeling that this woman was involved in some kind of murder, or attempted murder." I said, "Oh, really. Don't say anything. Thank you for telling me that. That can be helpful." We came back and we sat down, and we prayed. I looked at the woman and I said, "Just look at me now." She looked right at me with this frightening look in her eyes. There was something evil in her eyes. I said, "In the Name of Jesus Christ, I command any evil spirit who is bothering this woman to be gone right now." She just kept looking at me with this evil look, almost mocking. So I tried again. Nothing.

Usually whenever I was in a situation like this a prayer like that always worked, but this time it did not. So I tried from other angles, using different prayers. Nothing was working. Finally I decided I had to do something I was told never to do unless it's really necessary: Ask the spirit its name. Remember, now, the devil is a liar. You don't know what kind of an answer you're going to get, so you have to be careful. I had never done this before but I had seen it done, especially in Steubenville with the Bishop and the priest.

I said, "In the Name of Jesus Christ, I command you and any evil spirits bothering this woman tell me who are you. What is your name?" And from her mouth came the word, "Asmodeus."

Asmodeus is the devil in the Book of Tobit in the Bible who was killing off the husbands of Sarah. When Tobias wanted to marry Sarah he was told she had been married seven times and each time her husband died the night of the wedding. The one who was killing them was an evil spirit named Asmodeus.[32] This woman said she tried to kill her husband, so I thought this made sense. That's the evil spirit that was bothering her.

I said, "I command you, Asmodeus, in the Name of Jesus Christ to be gone from this woman, this sister of mine, this child of God. You be gone right now!" She just kept looking at me with this awful look and nothing was happening. Again, I tried.

I knew from experience that sometimes when I'm praying like this, it does help if I ask the Virgin Mary to help me. Because I also believe she was kept from all power of Satan through her Immaculate Conception, thanks to her Son, Jesus Christ. So I asked Mary to help me. And then all of a sudden a voice from her mouth said, "Can't you see that we are legion?" And I said, "Thank you, Lord, thank you God, thank you, Jesus. Now in the Name of Jesus Christ I command you legions of evil spirits, devils, all of you to be gone and away from this woman in the Name of Jesus Christ."

At this she pitched over forward and I had to catch her. I sat her back up in her place and her face started to change. Something came over her—peace, freedom and joy—I don't know what to call it. That demonic look in her eyes was gone. Right away I began to pray, as we always should, that the Holy Spirit would really fill her, fill the emptiness there now with the Spirit of God.

Here is a letter from this woman telling me how much her life had changed from that moment on and thanking me in glowing terms for having helped her to be free again:[33]

December 26, 1978
Father Leo,
> *Beloved, unforgettable Fr. Leo, the instrument of God, who was put into my life to heal me and free me from the heavy*

---

[32] Tobit 3:8 and 3:17.
[33] Reyna gave me permission to talk about her case and to use her name.

chains that had me bound for more than five years. How marvelous the ways of the Lord! You, Father Leo, gifted with the ineffable charism that I cannot explain, but that is effective, real and operative.

Let us praise the Lord Jesus, Glory to God, thanksgiving to him who can do all things! his Word, living and actual, is manifested through the ages in the same way that Jesus once freed the Gerasene man. My spiritual experience has been so profound, so intimate, so true, thanks to you and to your gift from on high, that I would be happy if it could serve as an example and an encouragement to other souls. Count on me if I can be of any help.

Reyna Frutos

Here again, there is so much to be learned from all this about the power of evil and the greater power of God to overcome every evil.

SISTER EMILIA

Another time, in July 1980, I was giving a weeklong retreat in Valladolid for 175 nuns from all over Spain. The first night I went over just to say hello to those who were arriving and one of the nuns came up to me and told me she had heard about my praying for someone whose arm had been healed. I said, "Oh yeah, thank God for that." There was a nun standing there named Emilia and she said, "You mean you pray for people to be healed and people are actually healed?" I said, "Well, that sometimes happens."

"Well, I'm happy to hear that because I'm not well. I'd love to be healed."

I said, "You're going to be here all week and I'm sure we can find time to pray. We'll be praying for everybody anyway."

"No, would you please pray for me now."

"Well, all right. Let's just slip into the chapel here." One of her sisters was there with her and she went in with us. I didn't know what her problem was and I didn't have a lot of time to ask her but I prayed over her and asked God to heal her.

The next day when I came back to begin the retreat with the sisters, she came up to me and said, "I did feel better last night after you prayed with me. But today I really feel worse." I said, "Well, I don't have a lot of time right now; let's say a prayer." I said a prayer with her but, of course, we had 175 nuns there and I had a lot of work to do.

On Wednesday afternoon we said we would have confession for anybody who was interested in receiving that Sacrament. So she came to me and said, "You know I felt a little better again after we prayed but then I got worse again."

I said, "I'll tell you what, Sister, sometimes the Sacraments are very helpful. Just receive absolution for all your sins here, and then when you go to Communion, you say at Communion, 'Lord, I am not worthy, but only say the word and I will be healed.' Say that and mean it. I think that would be very helpful. She said she would try that.

On Friday after dinner, she approached me again and said, "I'm getting worse all the time." By now I was suspecting that there was more to all of this than I understood and so I asked another priest to be with us the next time I saw her, which was later that evening.

When we got together again there were the two of us, another priest, and two sisters. I began by saying "Would you mind if I ask you a few questions? First of all, would you tell me a little bit about your problem?" I really didn't understand the problem too well because we had not had a lot of time to talk.

"It started about 15 years ago. I started getting these awful temptations that have to do with sex. I went to a priest and he said we all have temptations and not to worry. But the temptations were getting worse and I kept going back to see this priest who was a Jesuit and I'd tell him and after a while he said, 'you know I don't understand all this. Would you mind speaking to a psychiatrist?'"

She agreed to see the doctor because by this time she had stopped sleeping. She saw the psychiatrist several times but she only got worse and began having other problems such as rashes and lumps on her body. She showed me her arms where the rash was. She also said that she would vomit after eating. Finally, the psychiatrist suggested admission to a psychiatric hospital. After weeks of treatment, including medication, with no results she was released from the hospital. The doctors were baffled and could not think of anything else to do for her.

Years went by and the problem never got any better and, in fact, got worse. By now I knew there was something terrible going on with her. My first thought when she began her story was that there was some illness, perhaps a mental illness. But by now I was thinking something more drastic than that. I said, "I don't know what to say to you. I'm not even sure what to do. I've prayed with you several times. So let's just sit here in silence for a while and wait for God to give us an idea of what we need to do." So we sat there and closed our eyes. I said a prayer aloud: "Dear Lord, please help us now. Send your Spirit to help us understand what this is all about and what we should do."

All of a sudden, with her eyes closed, she began to speak, "Yes, there's something. There's something. Now I remember." So I opened my eyes and looked at her and she looked like she was talking in her sleep. I said, "Tell me, what was it?"

"Many years ago when I was eight years old, we lived in Cuba, and a man who was working for my father tried to rape me. I kicked him and scratched him and he didn't do anything." All this was said with her eyes closed as though she were sleeping. Then I asked, "Did it happen more than once?"

"Yes, but I would always manage to get away from him."

"Did you tell anybody?"

"No. I was afraid. I didn't know if they'd believe me, so I didn't tell anybody."

"Okay, anything else?"

"No, that's all."

I said, "Okay, thank you, and thank you, Lord, thank you, Holy Spirit." Then she opened her eyes and looked at me and said, "I had forgotten that completely. Why am I thinking of that now?" I said, "I don't know, Sister, but maybe God's trying to help us and let us know that somewhere, somehow, a door was opened." So I said, "Okay, now, let's pray." I said, "You look at me now. In the name of the Lord, Jesus Christ, I command any evil spirit that's bothering this sister of mine to be gone." Suddenly a voice yelled, "No." I said, "Yes, in the name of Jesus Christ you must go. You must leave her alone." Again there was a voice saying, "No." I said, "Yes." I kept on and the voice kept saying, "No." I'd say, "Jesus Christ is Lord," and the voice would scream, "No, No!" Finally, the voice began giving in and saying weaker each time, "No." I could tell I was winning. We were all winning. God was winning. So I asked Mary to help us, "In the Name of Jesus Christ I command you again any evil spirits to be gone from this sister." Then the voice said in a moaning voice, "Jesus Christ is Lord." And the sister's head fell back, her eyes started rolling around in her head.

I then prayed that the Holy Spirit would come and fill her. And she suddenly opened her eyes and said, "Oh, I feel so good. I am so happy." I looked at my watch; two hours had gone by and it was very late. I said, "I think now we must thank God and then I think we should all go to bed and get some rest." Since I was going home I said to the two nuns, "I want you to go with her. Don't leave her until she is in bed."

We walked out and the other priest said to me, "You know what? When you were praying in there and you were saying 'In the Name of Jesus Christ' and that voice was saying 'No,' I was really scared. But I'll never be afraid again because I realize that the more you prayed the more that voice was afraid of the name of Jesus Christ. I'll never be afraid again as long as

I have the name of Jesus Christ." I said, "That's what I hope everybody would do."

The next morning, as I came up the steps to the seminary where the retreat was, the three nuns were waiting for me. The nun we had prayed for said, "Wait till I tell you what happened. The sisters came with me. I got in bed and I looked at my clock on the table and it was 12:15. They put the light out and left. I closed my eyes and all of sudden, there was light in my eyes. I opened my eyes, and there was sun coming in through the window. It's the first time in 15 years that I have gotten a night's sleep. But that's not all. Look at my arms! All the rashes are gone. And the lumps on my body are all gone. When I went to breakfast, I started eating things that I used to vomit and my sisters, who had come with me, said, 'Hey, you can't eat those.' I said, 'Yes, I can. I'm not sick any longer. This is a new life.'"

This is a letter from her telling me what a new life she has:

Very dear Fr. Leo,

What joy to know we are united in the praise of God! What joy to be able to experience his great Love! How fortunate we are! He sees our misery, our littleness, our poverty and he fills us with his Love so that we can be witnesses to his greatness and his faithfulness. How good is our God!

Leo, I remember you so well, or better still, I remember that prayer team and that night of July 27 when the Lord manifested his greatness and his power and we felt his presence. Even now my heart jumps with joy and gratitude as I think of that night. I have no words to explain what I feel, but I can assure you that the Lord healed me spiritually and physically of EVERYTHING. He has changed my life in such a way that every year from now on I will celebrate the 27th of July as the day of my rebirth and of my new life in the Lord. Glory to him! Don't ever stop giving him thanks for using you the way he does to lead us all into praising him with so much joy.

Emilia

Later on, I met the Jesuit priest who had been her spiritual director for all those years. He said, "She's a changed woman." I feel so humble about all this. What would I do without Jesus Christ? Nothing at all would be possible. I would like every Christian, especially every priest, to understand what a power there is in the name of Jesus Christ and how Satan really is bothering us, in various ways—little ways and big ways. But with the name of Jesus Christ as our defender and shield, we never need be afraid of Satan. All you have to do is say, "Jesus Christ is my Lord" and he has to go away.

SATAN AND ME

I have had my own personal run-ins with Satan on two different occasions. When I entered into this kind of ministry, I would often have to lie down to take a nap because it is such exhausting work. On two occasions when trying to nap I felt like I had the weight of a whole house crushing me and it was so intense that I was trying to say a prayer and I was having a hard time opening my mouth. Finally, when I was able to say, "Jesus," the weight would go away. I know I wasn't asleep when these things happened and I know it wasn't my imagination. I am sure that it is Satan who is not happy with anything you do against him in the name of Jesus Christ.

Another thing I learned is that if I was going to do anything in this ministry, especially if I was going to speak to priests about this kind of thing, I always had to protect myself from the power of Satan, who did not want me to do God's work. As is often the case in life, I had to learn this the hard way and I can relate two occasions to illustrate this.

Once I was asked to give a talk to a group in a suburb of Madrid in a parish where I had never been before and where there were going to be several priests in attendance. I should have realized that I had to pray and protect myself against the power of Satan before I left but I didn't think of it. So, I started off to find this parish, in all the traffic of Madrid, and I got lost and stopped and asked directions and was sent in a certain direction and was lost again, and asked directions again and was sent in the opposite direction. I kept being sent from one place to another and couldn't find the church, and by the time I got there it was quite late and most of the priests had gone. There were still some people left to hear me but most of the priests had left because they thought I wasn't coming. Then I realized why it was that I was being sent in different directions by people. I really believe that Satan did not want me there that night.

Another time I was going to give a retreat for priests in Seville. I was taking a plane out of Madrid to go to Seville and I got to the airport, and could not get through the security control. I kept setting the alarm off, no matter how much I took out of my pockets, and took things off. Finally, the police couldn't understand what was going on and, I looked innocent enough, so they let me go. At the airport in Seville, my suitcase came out on the baggage carousel and when my satchel with my papers for the talks came out and it fell over and opened up. My papers started flying around the airport because there was a wind coming in from the outside. People were running around picking up my papers. I needed those papers and I couldn't figure out what was happening. And then, of course, it dawned on me that I was going to speak to priests. And I really think that retreat did a lot of good for several priests, from what I heard, and I should have known that Satan would not like that and he would do what he could to hinder me.

From these two experiences I've learned that when I'm going to do anything like that—and anytime really—we should always protect ourselves with a prayer to Jesus.

Several years ago, when my mother was still living, I would try to drive down to Massachusetts to see her once a week. One day, as I drove through the outskirts of one town, I noticed a night club advertising "Nude Dancing." I raised my right hand toward the building and said, "Jesus Christ is Lord of that building."

The next time I drove by, I repeated the same words and added, "I command any evil spirits using that building to be gone from there." I don't know how many times I said such words, but one day I drove by and saw that the building had burned down.

Needless to say, I have no way of knowing if my prayers and my commands in the name of Jesus were the cause of the building burning down. But I do believe that if all Christians began to pronounce Jesus as Lord of their lives, their homes and families, their towns and their country, we would see that it would make a real difference. Satan has power but we have a greater power in the name of Jesus Christ.

I say again that all this is a witness to the power of God, the goodness of God, the love of God, the power in the Name of Jesus Christ and the Holy Spirit and hoping it will help, especially priests who might read this. I want to repeat here that all I have told is for the praise and glory of God. Over and over I want to say: "You are my God, I thank you!"

AN OFFERING TO GOD

I will end with a story from a letter I had sent to my mother from Spain for Mother's Day in 1983. My sister, Anne Marie, had kept it all these years. Here is that story from the letter:

Dear Mom,
On Wednesday of Holy Week I was hearing confessions in a cloistered convent in Valladolid when a sister came in whom I had seen years before when she belonged to a community of

teaching sisters. I had gone to give a retreat in her convent and after the first talk she refused to come back and listen to me. She thought I was either crazy or fanatic. Later she entered this cloistered convent where she is now very happy...

She said, "Years ago I thought you were crazy. Now I envy you because you know Jesus so well. Can you help me to know him too?"

We talked for a long time. She had some objections and a lot of questions. She thought she didn't have enough faith, for one thing. I explained as best I could. She cried and still thought it was impossible for her to get to know Jesus. So I said, "Let's pray and let the Holy Spirit do what he wants." So I prayed with her.

Two days ago I went back to that same convent to hear confessions. She waited until all the others had finished and then came in. She said, "It's me; do you recognize me?" It's so dark in the confessional. I answered, "Yes." She asked if she could put the light on and read me something, but first she asked, "Are you really my friend and do you really want to help me?" I said, "Of course." So she started reading a letter she had written telling me what had happened after we had prayed together. I wish I had that letter here now. It was so beautiful.

First she said it had frightened her when I told her I loved her and wanted to help her. But then she said she understood what I meant because she knew I was a very holy man, (at least she thinks so!), and she sensed that Jesus was very close. She said she began to experience his presence while we were praying and afterwards she continued to feel him very close and she knew something was happening in her life.

That night, Holy Thursday, she was up praying until 4:00 in the morning and when she thought of going to bed, she couldn't. She just had to keep on praying. She went to the iron grille that separates the sisters from the altar and she knelt there looking up at the big, beautiful crucifix they have behind the altar. All of a sudden she began to cry and cry as she looked at the crucifix. But she said they were tears of joy because before she had been meditating on the Passion (it was now Good Friday, of course) but now she knew what Jesus was saying to her. He was saying, "Yes, Sister, I died for you but now I'm alive and I live on in you. You and I are one." And she knew this was true and she felt his presence as never before.

And she knew she had to be a saint. She couldn't be less than a saint because Jesus needed her to be a saint. And she wanted to offer herself as a Victim soul to suffer anything Jesus might want, and to die in any way and at any time that Jesus would want because now she had to live his life and only his. She had to allow him to live again and die again in her so that the world could be saved.

Now she is waiting for me to go and say a Mass at the convent and at that Mass she wants me to offer her up with the host on the paten so that from now on it will truly be Jesus, living, suffering and dying in her. That's her only wish.

All this is surprising when you know this sister. She is probably the last sister in the convent you would expect to talk like that. She has a great sense of humor and is not the least bit fanatic, or even overly pious. Remember, eight years ago she didn't want to listen to me because she thought I was a fanatic. Now, suddenly, she has met Jesus in a new way and is making giant strides in holiness. Praise God! Praise God! All this is sort of a Mother's Day gift to you. Hope you like it.

Love,

Leo

CONCLUSION

People who have heard these stories are under the mistaken impression that I am a holy man. But I know myself to be a miserable sinner. Only my conviction that God is loving and merciful saves me from despair. That's a funny thing about deepening your prayer life—you become more and more aware of how utterly unlike God, how flawed you are.

Saint Faustina Kowalska, that great apostle of God's mercy, wrote in her diary, #1107:

Today God gave me inner light and the understanding as to what sanctity is and of what it consists. Although I have heard these things many times in conferences, the soul understands them in a different way when it comes to know of them through the light of God which illumines it. Neither graces, nor revelations, nor raptures, nor gifts granted to a soul make it perfect, but rather the intimate union of the soul with God. These gifts are merely ornaments of the soul, but constitute neither its essence nor its perfection.

This illumination is my goal and it is the true vocation of every Christian. I'm still striving for this essence, which is union with God. If anything in these pages makes anyone yearn for that union and strive for it even a little more, then telling all this will have been worthwhile.

Finally, let us go back to the words of that Psalm: "Oh God, YOU are my God, I thank you."

Please pray for me!

Leo P. Maxfield, M.S.